GET INTO THE GROOVE
OF LIFE

RID YOURSELF OF STRESS AND ANXIETY, LIVE THE LIFE YOU DESERVE

MARTIN MORIARTY

CONTENTS

GET INTO THE GROOVE OF LIFE
CHECKLIST

(always start your day with a positive mind...)

This checklist includes:

- 5 items to help your day be positive

- The highest quality of stress free items

- Where you can buy these items for the lowest price

"It's time to start living the life you've imagined" - HENRY JAMES

To receive your free guide to the stress free life, visit the link below:

mmoriartylifesapeach.com

If at all possible, I'd ask that you leave a honest review on Amazon after you finish reading this book.

INTRODUCTION

"If people concentrated on the really important things in life, there'd be a shortage of fishing poles."

— *DOUG LARSON*

With the standards set by today's world, "livin' the dream" is often a joke that one cracks as they race off to their high-stress job. Upon arriving home with an aching neck, fatigue, and bills stacked as high as Mount Rushmore, it's no surprise that most of us resort to plopping down in a recliner to return to a simpler time by watching our old favorite TV shows. When an episode of *The Wonder Years* comes to a close and reality clicks back into place, it's quite easy to understand why your outlook appears to be...well, let's just say *bleak*.

If you find that talking to a therapist leaves you even more exhausted and confused than when you sat down with them, you might just be ready for a different kind of solution that can help you relieve stress and anxiety. Yet, you have no clue just what that solution can be, and maybe you've hit a brick wall, wondering if the solution is buried within some kind of unsolvable Morse code riddle.

Thankfully, the answer is far simpler, and it does not require the help of a leading trailblazer who has a thousand college degrees and proclaims to be an expert in human behavior. You just need this book that is already conveniently in your hands!

So, why bother reading yet another book about stress and anxiety? Aside from holding onto the time heals all wounds euphemism, you may not have many other options on the table (although, giving grandma a call does seem to help). Let's face it, though, you need practical solutions that can finally allow you to kick your stress and anxiety to the curb (just don't kick it too hard or you might shatter a window or your foot).

All jokes aside, this book offers eight, easy attainable ways to free yourself of the burdens that are weighing you down. Let go of the belief that life has to be a stress-inducing string of events from sunrise to sunset. All you need is to employ a handful of exercises and techniques, and once you do, you'll find that life can be quite luminous, if not downright amazing.

What you currently have is an out-of-balance lifestyle, and what you need is to find an equilibrium. Right now, you may feel like you are walking on a tightrope above a volcano of hot lava, sweating profusely as you attempt to step closer to your destination. This may be an exaggeration, but the statistical data on the stress levels in America are not. As evidenced in a *New York Times* article released in 2019, "Last year, Americans reported feeling stress, anger, and worry at the highest levels in a decade, according to the survey, part of an annual Gallup poll of more than 150,000 around the world" (Chokshi, 2019).

If those statistics aren't concerning enough, there is evidence that anxiety is stronger than ever as well. For instance, "Anxiety disorders are the most common mental illness in the U.S., affecting 40 million adults in the United States ages 18 and older, or 18.1% of the population every year" (Anxiety and Depression Association of America, n.d.). It's safe to say that we all need as many solutions as we can get, given that this appears to be an epidemic that doesn't seem to know when it's time to hit the brakes. But unlike the ghastly birthday gifts that arrive at your doorstep every single year, this is not a problem that can be thrust into the back of a closet.

You need an awareness of what problems or issues are contributing to your stress and anxiety. Admittedly, you may wish to launch all your problems into the nearest black hole that is floating through space (and maybe yourself), but alas, this is a technology that has yet to materialize for common use. There is always a reason that stress and anxiety are surging through your body, and with the help of this book, you can figure out why.

You will learn the triggers that are causing your undue burdens and how to find the practices and solutions that can work to lighten them. While you may never land on the front cover of a glossy magazine for your effort, you can, in fact, create a life that is unbelievably rare—unless, of course, you strike up a friendship with George Clooney, then maybe then you can finally get that striking photo of yourself on *People Magazine*. One can dream. But even if good ole' George never calls you back, a mind-body balance is still in the works for you.

The question is: *Can anyone achieve such a state of being where stress is wiped out forever?*

Well, it's a good thing you asked, because not only can you eradicate stress but you can also put an end to the barrage of negative thoughts and anxieties that have set up camp in your central nervous system. Not only is this bold objective possible, it is entirely feasible without the financial overhaul that equates to the dimensions of an African elephant. By which I mean, you don't need to spend a fortune to find peace.

Oh, and in case you're wondering, you won't need to invest in medication, either, but I'll understand if you decide to go ahead and get that foot massager that you've had your eye on—it may just help take the edge off. If that seems like a fair deal, then read on and prepare yourself for a radical makeover (this one won't require you to purchase a brand-new-you wardrobe, either. Though, I'm sure the one you have is as slick as John Travolta's hair from the movie *Grease*).

1

STRESS AND HOW IT AFFECTS THE BODY AND SOUL

"One of the best pieces of advice I ever got was from a horse master. He told me to go slow to go fast. I think that applies to everything in life. We live as though there aren't enough hours in the day but if we do each thing calmly and carefully, we will get it done quicker and with much less stress."

— *VIGGO MORTENSEN*

I f you've ever experienced the physical sensation of having a panic attack, you will know that it feels, quite literally, like your heart is about to burst out of your chest and stick to the ceiling like dried pancake batter. This is one of the single worst experiences that you can have as a result of stress, but before we get too far ahead of ourselves, let's look at stress that we all experience on a day-to-day basis. As stated by the Mental Health Foundation [MHF] (n.d.), "Stress can be defined as the degree to which you feel overwhelmed or unable to cope as a result of pressures that are unmanageable" (para. 1).

Let's use a narrative to help you better understand stress.

Picture this: Tony is in the kitchen with his wife, Katherine, who is about to come unglued because her Aunt Judy had the audacity to show up an hour early for Thanksgiving dinner without calling first. As you can imagine, this is about to get heated. Aunt Judy walks in waving her arms about, shooting off her opinions about how the table should be set. But she doesn't get very far in proclaiming her immaculate vision for the evening, because Katherine goes ballistic. Although Tony isn't ready to break out the divorce papers, he sure is ready to crack open a beer because this is a hefty load to heave on a single holiday.

If you think about it, this is how most people deal with stress: they will do anything they can to just forget about it, hence the reason why stress builds up and becomes a monumental problem.

But let's not be too hasty in declaring all stress is bad. The Aunt Judy type of stress is definitely bad, but other types of stress can offer some positives. Now, you might be wondering what on Earth I'm babbling about, and maybe you can't possibly imagine the good side to stress. Yet, here it is: The flipside of stress is that it can give you a leg up when you are faced with the pressure from your boss to take on an extra project or when you want to improve your running speed so that you can win the next marathon you'll be competing in. Stress can enhance your concentration, support your immunity, and help you conquer challenges like an iconic hero that you obviously are. (We're consulting with the mayor of Philadelphia to place a statue near the historic Liberty Bell on South 6th Street in your honor, so clear your schedule, since we'll need you to pose for it.)

Stress can even help you out when you are getting ready to go on a date, and it is what makes you excitedly want to bounce off the walls and what sends you running back and forth to the bathroom to check and recheck your hair while you are waiting for that magic moment of his or her arrival (while you dart off to the bathroom, flip on that once popular song by Jay and The Americans and you may just feel the allure stirring up inside).

Your true problems arise when this good stress sends your body into overdrive, and it leads to an endless overwhelming feeling. Before you know it your life is a frantic and scattered mess of thoughts and random actions that don't amount to much. This is what is known as chronic stress, and it can destroy your life if you let it. But before you plan out your upcoming appearance on

Dr. Phil to discuss how it all went wrong, know that there is a way to relieve bad stress and find your balance.

THE EFFECTS STRESS: HANGING BY A THREAD

There are a few areas in the body that generate the state of chronic stress over time: the amygdala, the hypothalamus, and the adrenal glands. If left unrestrained, these three can be like those juvenile teen delinquents that tear through a department store, yanking everything off the shelves, making light of the typhoon of debris trailing behind.

The chain of events starts with the amygdala, which detects the threat levels that exist around you. If danger is near, the amygdala blasts the mayday distress signal to tip off your hypothalamus that a crisis is reigning down. The hypothalamus then gives marching orders to the adrenal glands, and they dispense the adrenaline and cortisol hormones to prepare your body for war.

Meanwhile, the hypothalamus, with the help of the hormone epinephrine, then sends off a light beam to inform the rest of your body to enter into fight-or-flight mode (Healthline, 2017, & American Brain Society, 2019).

The resulting health problems are many (you better sit down, this might take a while). If that fight-or-flight mode doesn't switch off, you're in for some severe blows to your overall well-being. The range of effects you may endure include, but are, sadly, not limited to:

- heartburn
- depression
- insomnia
- high blood sugar and pressure
- low sex drive
- fertility problems
- memory problems
- learning and cognition problems (Healthline, 2017, & American Brain Society, 2019)

To illustrate these points more specifically, "Frequent or chronic stress will make your heart work too hard for too long. When your blood pressure rises, so too do your risks for having a stroke or heart attack" (Healthline, 2017). (If that doesn't make you want to sprint off to the nearest yoga class and discover your inner zen, I don't know what will.)

Everyone has varying responses to stress and will react differently as a result. You know the contrast between low stress and extreme stress levels in your personal life.

Say, for example, you are driving home, but you miss your turn onto your street. You might feel frustrated for a moment, but then your favorite song comes on the radio and you forget about it almost instantly. This is a low-stress event.

A high-stress event would be if you are tearing down the hallway of an airport because you are late for your flight. You rush over to your terminal, bags in tow, and your head is pounding like there is a jukebox behind your temples blasting the greatest grunge rock hits of the 90's. You look up just in time to see the glowing red lights declaring your public humiliation: FLIGHT DEPARTED. Your heart sinks to the floor, dragging behind you as you trudge toward the front entrance to flag down a taxi. Your imagination kicks into high gear as you realize the domino effect that this one miscalculation will cause on the week ahead.

If you can't get a handle on low- and high-stress events, you can face problems in these four areas: cognitive, emotional, physical, and behavioral (Help Guide, 2020). When you experience the red flag stress response over and over again and are unable to shake it off (like Taylor Swift proclaims we must), then you know that your body is telling you that it's time to do something different. Spot the warning signals below when they arise.

Cerebral

These symptoms can be an interference to intellectual perfor-mance as well as an impairment to proper psychological func-tioning:

- poor recollection
- persistent negative outlook
- lack of concentration
- apprehensive or rapid thoughts (Help Guide, 2020)

Emotions and Impressions

The following symptoms pertain mainly to feelings and how they color the view of the world at large as well as personal surroundings:

- hopeless or despondent demeanor
- temperamental backlash
- perpetual overwhelm
- tendency to alienate from others
- debilitating anxiety (Help Guide, 2020)

Physical and Visceral Sensations

The symptoms listed below are the body's way of exhibiting the degree to which the body is in distress:

- soreness or throbbing
- chest pain or accelerated heart rate
- recurring illness
- queasiness or vertigo (Help Guide, 2020)

Behavioral Tendencies and Ways of Coping

The below behaviors are ways that people cope with stress, and they are unhealthy, yet are often overlooked as serious issues that negatively impact someone's lifestyle:

- increased or decreased food consumption
- procrastination or avoiding obligations
- sleeping a lot or a little
- turning to stimulants to ease stress (Help Guide, 2020)

CAUSES OF STRESS

There is a scene from *The Office* where Dwight decides the best course of action to prepare his co-workers for a fire is to pretend that one is actually happening. His privy arrangement elicits a full-blown panic among the team as everyone scrambles to find a safe exit out of the building. When it appears that they are trapped and running out of options for escape, the hysteria sets in. As the terror continues to heighten, Stanley collapses to the ground due to the overload of stress, and his underlying heart condition doesn't help matters much at all. While this scene induces a few chuckles, it does also highlight the very real causes of stress that can happen to anyone (Lieberstein & Blitz, 2009).

Everyone has a different response to stress, as the example above shows, as some characters in the scene were panicked but still searching for a solution while others, like Stanley, lost consciousness because the stress was too much to handle.

The causes of stress are diverse and they include: work, personal life issues, internal perceptions, such as fear, unexpected changes, and traumatic events—to name a few. It's clear that we often don't have helpful responses to stress or the awareness that the way that we are reacting needs to shift. Stress is an epidemic in our culture, and while we have handy tools at our fingertips, we are programmed to hurry through our days as if we are still on the high school track team and the coach is barking out orders to run faster with a stopwatch in hand.

Run! Run! Run!

This sad state of affairs leads to an entire country that quite often doesn't know how to deal with everyday stressors, much less deep anguish.

According to Scott (2020), "Americans now spend 8% more time at work compared to 20 years ago and about 13% of people work a second job. At least 40% report their jobs are stressful, and 26% report they often feel burned out by their work" (para. 7). These statistics alone show that if you are overburdened by your job, you are certainly not alone. Work has become the main focus of our days as we attempt to get ahead and often fall short.

Even if it is suppressed, there are people in your life that are stressed out about their jobs and lives and are looking for some sign that you feel the same way that they do.

Stress On The Job

Finding stable employment is one thing, but finding and keeping a job that is both fulfilling and pays the bills is challenging. The average American, typically, finds themself in a job that allows them to get by.

Common job stress inducers are:

- being dissatisfied with your job
- discrimination in the workplace
- excessive workload
- unsatisfactory bosses
- working extended hours
- unsafe work environment
- limited promotions or fear of being let go (WebMD, 2020)

Personal and Individual Stress

Establishing a happy personal life is not only an ambitious goal, for some it can feel quite impossible. When both work and home life are out of control, a sudden change of events can send any sensible person spiraling downhill into the void of a gloomy mentality.

Common personal, every-day stressors include:

- moving into a new residence
- dealing with a recurring illness or injury
- divorce or separation
- death of a family member
- taking on new financial responsibilities
- getting married
- getting laid off or fired (WebMD, 2020)

Relationship Strain

If you ever had a fight with your wife or husband, then you know how stressful that can be. But there are other super downers that can do a song-and-dance in your relationships, including:

- lack of quality time together
- decrease in affection or sex
- poor communication
- too much alcohol or drug use
- abusive or dominating behavior with one or both partners
- lack of balancing shared responsibilities (Scott, 2020)

Frantic Lifestyle

Remember Dolly Parton singing about working 9 to 5? Yeah, man, what a dream that was. Your day seems to go from sunup to sundown. A frantic lifestyle can make you feel:

- as though there is not enough time
- strained by having to juggle two occupations
- weary of so many social expectations
- like you are neglecting self-care
- downtrodden about mishaps of minor setbacks (Scott, 2020)

Life Of A Parent

There isn't anything you wouldn't do for your child, but sometimes you wish it were a tad easier and that there weren't so many Cheerios to clean up. The life of a parent comes with:

- hectic schedules
- maintaining a home
- tense parent-child relationships
- possibly bringing up a child with disabilities
- low salaries
- possibly sole custody of children
- marital or relationship controversies (Scott, 2020)

Financial Pressures and Decisions

Money makes the modern world go around and creates a merry-go-round of stress in you, including:

- the guilt of spending money on unnecessary items
- disagreements over how to handle money
- worries or anxieties over financial debt or monthly bills
- fear of late payments, overdrawn accounts, or bankruptcy
- apprehension over discussing financial matter with a debt collector
- lack of financial mastery leading to poor monetary resources (Scott, 2020)

Personal Identity Traits

Like Lady Gaga says, "Baby, I was born this way." And while that can be empowering, sometimes people are just predisposed to feel more stress and anxiety, such as:

- extroverts, who feel the strain over the absence of social connections
- introverts, who can be stressed out over lack of solitude
- perfectionists, who feel the strain of attachment to specifications

- extremely self-reliant individuals, who feel resistant of asking for help
- intellectuals, who may feel out-of-place in a culture of vivacious gatherings
- the humorists, who may experience being misperceived as lacking depth (Scott, 2020)

ANXIETY AND STRESS: WEIGHING THE DISTINCTION

Meet Veronica! She has a dazzling smile and long black hair, and she is a well-respected veterinarian. She often handles the most difficult surgeries at the clinic, and this past week was especially taxing.

She had to do four emergency operations on dogs, and on top of that, her best friend was in a car accident. Even though she has the weekend off, she can't sleep or relax, and everything is pushing her closer to her breaking point. Earlier today her husband asked her if she'd like to make French toast with him, she furrowed her brow, flattened her lips into a straight line, and stomped off to the bedroom slamming the door. As you might have guessed, Veronica's temper is due to high levels of stress; although, she *would* say that it's due to her husband's ignorance.

The mounting stress at work coupled with her friend's car accident has forged an emotional response that is the equivalent to the agitation that some may feel during a midlife crisis, which I'm sure you never experienced before (wink, wink).

In contrast, we will now take a look at Jeffrey, who is dealing with a different kind of emotional response: anxiety. Jeffrey fears that he is going to be diagnosed with heart disease because it runs in the family, even though his doctor has reassured him that his heart is healthy. Jeffrey finds himself frantically searching online for anything that can prevent the arrival of his untimely death.

His family worries about him because he has an unwarranted compulsion to research and discuss heart conditions of every kind. It's quite obvious that Jeffrey experiences a substantial load of symptoms as a result of his anxiety, not his presumed heart condition. Jeffrey typically experiences insomnia, fatigue, and muscle tension due to his excessive worrying.

The above examples only illustrate two of the many ways that stress and anxiety can manifest as particular responses. Even though your reactions to stress may not be as extreme as Veronica or Jeffery, you could still be dealing with the significant toll that these emotional responses can yield. You could be moving through your days and suddenly be hit with ongoing fatigue that leaves you feeling like you've been popping sleeping pills at the start of the day.

On the other hand, you may discover that you are faced with ongoing insomnia that gives you no option but to finally delve into *The Lord of The Rings,* which has been sitting on your bookshelf since 1998. Even though Bilbo Baggins has become one of your favorite midnight companions, you would like to regain your ability to complete at least one REM cycle. Without the proper awareness, you might not have any idea that the cause of these intrusions and sleeplessness may just be stress or anxiety (Alvord & Halfond, 2019).

The main distinction between anxiety and an anxiety disorder is that the former will not interfere with the functioning of your everyday existence and the latter will (Medical News Today, 2020). Stress is usually brought on by an outside source, while anxiety is typically rooted in internal triggers. It's quite common that stress will fade once the problem has been solved. Anxiety, on the other hand, is incredibly persistent in its nature and is not resolved simply because the dilemma has found a resolution.

There is nothing abnormal about having anxiety; it is a natural human response to distress. In fact, anxiety can be quite helpful. Say, for example, you are riding your bike and a deer leaps out in front of you, and you jerk your handlebars in the direction of a bubbling creek. You're soaking wet and so is your bike, but your spinal cord remains intact and the deer is just fine. (Thank goodness. I was worried for Bambi for a moment.)

You decide to pocket this story for when Uncle Gerald comes over for Christmas and tries to pretend that his jokes are funnier than yours. So, in this case, anxiety not only saves you a fatality, but it will prove to have positive long-term results for many family celebrations to come! Take that, Uncle Gerald!

Anxiety only becomes abnormal when it is unrelenting and impedes the natural flow of life events. An anxiety disorder will absorb so much of one's energy, there is almost none left for daily activities. Anxiety itself can be perplexing and unpleasant, but it will often dissolve as the day transpires. The main thing to remember here is that when anxiety seems to be taking over your life, you likely have a disorder on your hands.

If you find that the only anxiety you feel is when you are placing your order with the local pizza parlor while your kids are yelling loudly about how there *really* is a *dead squirrel* in the backyard, then it's fair to say that you are in the clear.

If there seems to be an anxiety disorder at play, there are four central afflictions we will cover here: general anxiety disorder, panic disorder, phobias, and social anxiety.

1. **General anxiety disorder** is when you experience alarming fear having to do with major circumstances, objects, or prospective happenings. You experience heightened irritability, complications with getting restful sleep, unmanageable apprehension, struggles

with sustained focus, an inability to remain calm, and a tendency toward agitation. (Medical News Today, 2020)

2. **Panic disorder** is characterized by repeated panic attacks that may be brought on by a formidable experience or excessive stress levels. Panic attacks could very well be prompted without an obvious cause as well. A panic attack is a piercing awareness of fear that shocks the body into abrupt and present moment feelings of dread and horror. These attacks will typically reach their climax and come to an end after approximately ten minutes, but they can be drawn out for several hours. (Medical News Today, 2020)

3. **Phobias** are an illogical fear of a particular item, setting, venture, or task. This fear causes an extreme avoidance of the trigger so as to attempt to uphold a sense of composure. Phobias are unambiguous because they can be linked to a clear dawn of inception. What is not so clear is finding a way to iron out a solution to putting an end to the severity of the psychological agony. (Medical News Today, 2020 & Healthline 2018)

4. **Social anxiety** is characterized by a fear of being criticized, mocked, or facing some type of negative or harsh disapproval. Social anxiety can occur in a small group, in a community environment, or one on one. The reason this disorder is concerning is because it can

reach a point of disturbance where the individual is unable to leave the house or will simply go to extreme measures to dodge social interactions. (Medical News Today, 2020)

Anxiety: Origins and Signs

The definite causes of anxiety are still a mystery; however, there is substantial evidence as to the plausible reasoning behind these disruptions in consciousness.

Causes

1. **Genetics** is believed to be one of the contributing factors in the development of anxiety, as it can be passed down the family lineage you were born into. (Medical News Today, 2020 & Healthline Editorial Team, 2017)

2. **Medical factors** are an area of concern because anxiety can be brought on as an element of a distinct ailment, the side effects of a prescribed drug, or the turbulence after a medical procedure. (Medical News Today, 2020)

3. **Brain chemistry** is given a significant emphasis because the foundational belief in psychology research is that anxiety is an imbalance in hormones or nerve functioning. (Medical News Today, 2020)

4. **Personality type** is a consideration given that some people just so happen to be born with more anxiety issues than others. Those who have greater attachments to things having to be a certain way are adding to their existing stress, which then increases their chances of bringing on a personal struggle with anxiety. (Healthline, 2016)

5. **Trauma** is also a cause of anxiety as it can create triggers that were not there before the horrific events occurred. This could be trauma from an accident, a war zone, abuse, a health crisis, or the sudden death of a loved one. (Medical News Today, 2020 & Healthline Editorial Team, 2017)

THOUGHTS TO END WITH

Now that we've explored the ways that stress and anxiety can affect your body and your spirit, you should feel a little more confident about tackling these issues. Your physical body has definitely taken a hit, and it's impacting you on every level. The good news is that you have a better idea of what's causing your stress and what you can do about it. You can also see the difference between anxiety and stress, as they both show up in your life.

Since you have all this information at your disposal, you may be wondering what's next. It's not enough to know the symptoms and causes of your anxiety and stress, you also need to know how to properly deal with them.

The rest of the book will help you to recognize what needs to be removed from your life in order to decrease your stressors. You will then learn what to add into your life to lift your mood and keep your energy strong. Remember, you have what it takes to overcome your anxiety and stress. You just need to utilize the right tools and the right frame of mind to get you there.

If you find it helpful, keep a highlighter nearby so that you can refer back to the concepts that stood out to you. You can also use this as a permanent resource after you finish reading so that you can continue with the exercises listed throughout the book.

Reading the book is one thing, but putting what you learn into action will be key in achieving the transformation you are looking for. I trust that you will find the information contained within these pages to be invaluable on your journey to overcoming stress and anxiety.

2

DECLUTTER YOUR WAY TO STRESS RELIEF

"Staying positive doesn't mean you have to be happy all the time. It means that even on hard days, you know that better ones are coming."

— *UNKNOWN*

If you've ever found yourself in the home of a messy friend, trying your best to smile through your internal horror as you take in piles of clothes, dirty dishes, and old take-out containers, then you know how stress-inducing clutter can be. And that's not even taken into account the stress your friend must be under! Even if this friend of yours doesn't have a hoarding disorder, the untidiness is detrimental to their overall well-being. It seems that when it comes to structuring our days, most opt for professional advancement at the expense of personal welfare, such as, you know, doing something about those sweaty gym shorts from last week that smell so bad they need to be torched.

There seems to be a pervasive belief that progress means tossing aside essential needs in favor of a substitution that can, in no way, make up for the loss. The outcome is not advancement but hindrance amongst a mass pileup of scattered belongings along with jumbled priorities.

Your brain can only handle so much input in a day before it enters into overdrive or shuts down altogether. You can either be a runaway truck or a truck that has hit a wall, neither of which, I think you'll agree, are great choices. The key is to limit and organize both your mental and physical space so that you can put your energy toward productive tasks or feelings. By committing to maintaining the organization of your space, you are, in effect, grounding your sense of control over your days. You are the captain of the ship, and no ship sails if it's loaded down with junk!

When taking in your environment and the tasks ahead, there is a natural calmness that you carry when you are in a tidy home and office. Survey your ship! Look how clean and well-prepared it is for the journey ahead.

The goal of decluttering is to reduce your stress and anxiety levels. You don't need to hire Martha Stewart to come over and keep your home in perfect order (although, if that's an option, go for it). It's important to try your best to declutter and have a system that works well to create a sense of peace in your home and workspace.

But this decluttering process doesn't end with your external surroundings. It's also crucial that you carry that sense of peace over to your daily schedule. If you have 35 sticky notes shoved into your planner along with scribbles of tasks that you wrote out in a panic, it's time to employ a new system that will help you stay on track and keep you rock-solid like a Chevy pickup (you know, "Like a rock," and oh, sorry for getting that song stuck in your head). When you carve out the time to write out a well-organized plan for the day ahead, you take a lot of the guesswork out of the process. As you move from task to task, you will discover that things can flow quite seamlessly.

It is important to recognize that there are habits that you've stuck with for years that will need to be uprooted like an old tree stump and replaced for improved efficiency. It can be incredibly difficult to be open to an entirely new way of approaching your home and work routines. Transformation does not happen as quickly as you would like it to but if you stay with the process, you will not go back to old habits. You were able to shake that needy ex, so I think you can shake off old habits, too.

THE BENEFITS THAT AWAIT YOU

To help you understand just how important decluttering is and what fantastic advantages there are to living in an organized way, here are the many benefits:

- lower risk of depression
- decrease in stress
- improved energy levels and better sleep
- healthier relationships
- dedicated workout routine
- reduction of cortisol levels
- better diet choices
- weight loss (Fowler, n.d.)

So, you see, not only will you sleep, eat, and feel better, you will also up your tally of double takes as you strut through your favorite bar. Also, expect an influx of phone numbers slid your way.

Your home should be a place where you can unwind from the events of the day. For many of us, home is definitely not where the heart is. Home is where our stress breeds and multiplies like mice in the attic (show of hands, any good mice-in-the-attic stories?). As Fowler (n.d.), indicated in a study done by *Personality and Social Psychology Bulletin*, "Women who described their homes as 'cluttered' or 'full of unfinished projects' were more depressed, fatigued, and had higher levels of the stress hormone cortisol than women who felt their homes were 'restful' and 'restorative'" (Fowler, n.d.).

Do you ever wonder why you feel better after making your bed? Well, that's because it looks nice when it's made, and it makes you feel good that you accomplished the task. Those warm and fuzzy feelings can carry over into your sleeping patterns. As Fowler emphasized in a survey conducted by the National Sleep Foundation, "People who make their beds every morning are 19 percent more likely to report regularly getting a good nights' rest" (Fowler, n.d.). You know the subtle satisfaction that comes with sleeping between crisp sheets versus the not-so-subtle disappointment of crawling into bed and getting a good whiff of stale body odor assaulting your senses and feeling some crumbs from your previous late-night snacks. There really is nothing worse than staring at the ceiling wondering what your life has come to that you no longer carve out time to wash the sheets.

We can't all be like Donna Reed, dishing out pies on the daily while also maintaining a sparkly home and a whimsical smile. However, we all need to come home to a peaceful space that gives way to true relaxation.

Forgoing serenity in your home will result in an ever-growing list of intolerable burdens. You will find that accomplishing your goals is a seemingly impossible bar to reach like you're a gymnast who fails to grasp one of those uneven bars when doing a double twist and lands face first on the mat. As suggested by Fowler's reference to the *Journal of Neuroscience*, "Clutter is distracting, and research confirms that it can actually affect your ability to focus: Looking at too many things at once overloads your visual cortex and interferes with your brain's ability to process information" (Fowler, n.d.).

On top of regaining your focus, you will also find that a box stuffed with glazed donuts will lose its appeal (unbelievable, but true). The less stress that you face, the less likely you are to shove down unhealthy carbs like a hungry, hungry hippo. Typically, eating habits like this arise when our lives are loaded up with every imaginable stressor, which compels us to ignore our biological instincts for healthy foods. Fowler highlights this well by stating, "When you're organized, you're more likely to plan your meals, stock up on nutritious foods, and prep things like fruits and vegetables" (Fowler, n.d.).

On the same note, removing unnecessary distress has the appeal of spicing up and expanding your social circle. Strong evidence has demonstrated that "Disorganization can lead to shame and embarrassment and actually create a physical and emotional boundary around you that prevents you from letting people in" (Fowler, n.d.). Just think of your friend with the clutter from above. It's possible you are their only friend. And that's kind of sad. Denying the natural desire to invite friends over transforms your home into a prison, and I recommend that if you need a good dose of prison life, *The Shawshank Redemption* is the place to start. Crack open a few bottles of wine and invite some friends over while you're at it, but clean up first; you're not a prisoner to clutter.

You can expect to see an improvement in your fitness goals by organizing your home, office, and your schedule as well. By staying on top of your priorities, you will no doubt find that working up a sweat is more than just about heart health. Keeping everything in order will increase your willpower to build your endurance, strength, and the likelihood that you may be able to lift a car above your head someday. (That last one may never come in handy, but it could be the just the thing to land you an interview on *The Tonight Show with Jimmy Fallon.*)

Being disciplined enough to keep to a steady rhythm with your exercise goals will dramatically alter the future of your health for the best. Fowler indicated a study done by the *Journal of Obesity*, which states that "People who set short-term goals, have a plan, and record their progress are more likely to stick with an exercise program than those who show up at the gym and wing it" (Fowler, n.d.).

The impact of being organized can have some impressive results in your professional career. It's important to recognize that the quality of your work environment leads to quality decisions that will circle back to impact your productivity. When you are stressed, you are less proficient in your tasks, and you will naturally find yourself reaching for a tasty treat to alleviate the tension. This temporary fix will lead to more stress and ongoing poor decision-making, so let's call that the circle of not-so-great life. According to Fowler, the *Journal of Psychological Science* performed a study which indicated that "People who worked in a neat space for 10 minutes were twice as likely to choose an apple over a chocolate bar than those who worked in a messy office for the same amount of time" (Fowler, n.d.).

An apple over chocolate?!?

Madness, you may think, but take a moment to imagine yourself doing just that, and then imagine how much better you would feel about yourself and choices and how that will make you feel better about your work! This is the circle of life that you want, and it all begins with decluttering.

CLEARING OUT THE MESS FROM YOUR DWELLING SPACE

The first place to begin when you're trying to get a handle on your organization is to decide which part of your house you would like to focus on. It may be best to begin with a room that causes you the least amount of stress. Conquering a small hill gives you the courage to take on Mount Everest.

If you notice anything on the floor that clearly belongs in a fire pit, toss it. Any object that can be donated should be placed in a pile and prepare for the genuine satisfaction of releasing things you haven't touched since Clinton was in office. After your floors look spick and span, you can bring your attention to any surface in the room. Repeat the same process of making piles to donate, throw away, or hold onto (McCormick, n.d.).

As you are making these important decisions, be honest with yourself about why you want to keep an item. You may feel tempted to keep the sweater that Aunt Charlotte got for your birthday six years ago even though you've never worn it because it's just that ugly. The stabbing guilt that you feel is overpowering, but the burden of clutter that you carry is far worse. It's unlikely that Aunt Charlotte will even question you about the location of the ugly sweater (unless she is an investigative journalist, then you may want to have a believable story about how a gust of wind robbed you of the opportunity to wear the sweater ever again) (McCormick, n.d.).

Aside from the ugly sweater debacle, there will be many items that you will be tempted to keep that you never use. Avoid keeping anything that you tell yourself you might use someday (that's a lie, sadly, and you know it), and instead, keep the things that already provide you with value. Once you've decided what you would like to save, go ahead and organize them so that everything is neatly tucked away. If you take this decluttering process room by room, you will find that it is far less overwhelming than trying to tackle it at once (McCormick, n.d.).

Remember, even a linebacker only tackles one guy at a time. You won't be able to tackle the entire starting lineup of the New England Patriots at once. You got to take those guys down one by one.

One of the most daunting tasks is to take on clearing out the closets, as they are the magical realm of forgotten things. Just think what that wardrobe in *The Lion, The Witch, and The Wardrobe* led to! Maybe you even stuffed items so deep in the closet with the hope of never having to see them again. Closets have so many layers of distant memories, dreams, and hairdos that now belong to the newest collection of Awkward Family Photos. Plus, you never know just how many night crawlers will come springing out of the darkness only to land inches away from you. It's no wonder why most of us dismiss the idea of decluttering and instead find ourselves racing off to stock up on discount shoes (McCormick, n.d.). Yet, cleaning out a closet is an important step in decluttering, and you brave knight must take on the task. Just have a bottle of bug spray handy.

The next area to hone in on would be your drawers. Much like closets, it is a human tendency to shove belongings inside until the drawer no longer opens due to the sheer weight capacity. Overloading these spaces that we have daily contact with is only adding to the stress. Take the time to repeat the process of placing items into the donate, keep, or throw away categories. Always aim to eliminate items that you have not used in the previous 6 to 12 months. It's unlikely that you will miss the defective hole puncher that hardly works anymore (McCormick, n.d.).

CLEARING OUT THE MESS AT YOUR JOB

Since your desk is the spot where you spend most of your time at work, you can begin there. Remove everything off the desk and place them into different categories on the floor. Open all the drawers (while resisting the urge to panic at the sight) and sort the miscellaneous junk and actual important junk into categories as well. Trash the items or papers that you don't need and neatly organize all the things that you need to put back into the drawers. Be sure that every item has a specific location just as you did at home (McCormick, n.d.).

It is important to have a strong filing system at work so that your papers are where you can find them. There's nothing quite as embarrassing as having your boss ask you for a file and stand there impatiently as you haphazardly bulldoze your desk in search of it. The best thing you can do is maintain this system as papers come your way so that they are not littering your desk like snowflakes on your windshield in December. Floating, loose papers with no organization make a workspace intolerable as if attempting to accomplish a task in the middle of an apocalypse. Save yourself the headache (and the high dosage of Five Hour Energy shots). Keeping your desk clear has a way of limiting scattered thoughts and, therefore, scattered work (McCormick, n.d.).

Your computer is another point of stress, as you likely have thousands and thousands of emails in your inbox and a haphazard filing system on your desktop computer. Go through and delete files and emails that you don't need. Remove computer programs that you never use and desktop icons that cover your screen and make it look like a page from *Where's Waldo?*. Create a system for your emails and your files and sort everything that you need to access. Once you do this, make it a point to put emails and files into these folders throughout the day as you work. This process may be as appealing as swallowing cough syrup, but once you do it, you'll find that your stress at work rapidly declines (McCormick, n.d.).

One of the greatest hindrances to your productivity at work is the constant buzz of notifications on your computer and your phone that are akin to a blanket of mosquitoes hovering around you. Make it a point to eliminate unnecessary social media and news updates. Silence the ones that you want to be informed about until you can carve out time to review them on your break. No matter how demanding the world can be, you have to reign in the unending influx of information that comes your way; otherwise, you will be consumed by the tsunami. Some things just aren't worth your time or energy, being picky is necessary to achieve an uncluttered work life (McCormick, n.d.).

REARRANGING YOUR PERSONAL LIFE

Sit down and evaluate your personal and professional commitments by writing them all down on a piece of paper. Rate each one by how important it is to you and how much positivity it offers to your life. I think the old fashioned one to five scale is perfect for this. Consider how much time you are putting into the things that are important to you (these are your five-star commitments) versus things that are not adding anything to your life (one star, insert sad trombone music here). Cut out the things that have low scores and think about how this can free up your time to focus on things that are valuable to you. A good way to rate these commitments is to prioritize things that you love and remove the apparent priorities that add very little happiness to your life (McCormick, n.d.).

An important part of all this is becoming comfortable with saying "no" and disappointing some people in your life. Learning to manage this discomfort will cut out much of the stress that you are holding onto. Clinging to certain priorities out of a fear of letting others down is a sheer waste of time and only burns you out faster. If someone comes to you inviting you to some event that doesn't have you feeling jazzed, then decline the offer. Prepare for odd looks and drawn out silence but stand your ground; your time is yours alone (McCormick, n.d.).

Social etiquette can still have a place in your life while you hold fast to what is important to you. You'll learn that no one is going to kick down your front door because you utilized your freewill by not going to Stacey's birthday party. If you say "yes" to everything, you end up saying "no" to things that matter the most. Don't live somebody else's life because you're too afraid to live your own. (And it's okay to disappoint Stacey, as you're not even that great of friends in the first place.)

The next step is building yourself a routine. Now, you may be resistant to this, especially if you imagine a routine is like the movie *Groundhog Day.* (Who wants to live the same day over until they die? Not Bill Murray, that's for sure.) The picture that you have in your mind is probably quite depressing, but a routine doesn't have to feel exactly the same each day.

What matters is that you are creating consistency that allows you to be productive and gives you space to set your work aside at the end of the day to unplug. A routine ingrains habits into your subconscious until you find that certain priorities that were once a struggle are now far easier to accomplish. Rather than feeling tied down, you feel grounded (pun intended) in what's important (McCormick, n.d.).

Without a routine, your daily schedule will feel like a game of Whack-A-Mole, and that is pure torture to the human psyche. You probably find that you are all over the place, not truly accomplishing your tasks, but feeling like you ran 36 miles by the end of the day.

If you've ever heard of the phrase "work smarter, not harder," that's what I'm talking about. By planning out your day and week ahead of time, you're hitting predetermined targets. You don't have to waste time feeling disheveled because you are trying to complete random obligations and wondering where you should be investing your time.

There are few things in life that are more satisfying than bringing order back into your life (a warm slice of pecan pie is climbing the charts, though). By creating a plan and sticking to it, you are committed to ridding your life of unnecessary stress, anxiety, and wasted time.

One of the best ways to reclaim order in your life is to create a structure that is known as batching, which, yes, sounds super weird. But what I mean by this is that you group your tasks in bunches like bananas. For example, run all of your errands in one day. You could also prioritize similar tasks at work in the morning, such as meetings, and spend the afternoon focused on tasks that keep you on the computer (McCormick, n.d.).

By choosing to batch your days, you will find that you spend less time trying to reorient yourself as you switch gears. You don't have to be a ping-pong ball subjected to world champion ping-pong masters. It takes a lot more energy to go from emails to meetings, and then back to emails.

Consider doing this in every area of your life and find ways to batch together tasks that naturally belong together. You will find that you have more time on your hands to do things that help you unwind. The problem most people have is not that they don't have enough time but that there isn't enough consistency or structure to their time (McCormick, n.d.). Batching can help you become a pro at time and task management. Imagine yourself as a lion tamer in full control of the wild beast that is time, but don't put your fingers too close to those jaws.

On the personal side, the friends that you hold onto are just as important as the priorities you keep. If you have friends who leave you scratching your head wondering why you're friends to begin with, then you may need to evaluate the relationship. I mean, is Frank, the guy who eats raw hot dogs for breakfast really who you want to spend your limited time with? I don't know. Maybe you like raw hot dogs, too. If not, it's time to think about letting Frank find some friends who he can really enjoy those hot dogs with.

Your time is too valuable to waste on people who hold you back from your goals and your highest ambitions. When you are around people who motivate you and push you to be a better person, you will see that this is exactly who you become (Scott, 2020 & Creel, n.d.). So, don't become a raw hot dog eater just because your friend is one, as I know you can be so much more. You just need friends that can help you get there.

It can be hard to give yourself time to unwind from the day's activities. If you want to be more productive, you have to learn to make time for things that replenish your energy. Being in go-go-go mode has a way of making you feel as though you've been hit by a semitruck. You need to reflect on the things that really make you happy and put them into your schedule just like any other priority. Having things to look forward to can motivate you to really get things done. No routine should cut you off from things that give you true pleasure; life's too short for that (Scott, 2020 & Creel, n.d.).

A good practice to slip into your schedule is to have a morning and evening routine. You may be surprised by the sheer number of benefits that these practices have to offer. In the morning, you can take some time to quietly drink a cup of coffee, eat your breakfast, and calmly look over the day's priorities. It may seem a little woo-woo, magical thinking, but starting the day off peacefully will set the tone for a day of less stress and more productivity. I promise your cousin Alice who is always going on about mystical thinking and urging you to create a mood board isn't fully off the mark. But don't worry, you don't have to get into crafting (unless you want to, that is, no judgments here). When you end the day, also take time to plan out the next day's schedule so that you are ready to dive in at the start of your day with confidence (Scott, 2020 & Creel, n.d.).

You may notice that your productivity is hindered because a certain task gives you anxiety or a part of your day has you feeling overstressed. You need to do the work of figuring out why these things make you feel like an earthquake is happening in your gut. Once you understand where the anxiety is coming from (maybe a past mistake still haunts you like that doll from *The Conjuring*), then you can flip a mental switch in your brain that allows you to resolve these automatic, stressful responses. Doing this internal rearranging then leads to a more productive life (Scott, 2020 & Creel, n.d.).

Aside from a few intellectual and personal development giants out there, it seems that most of us lead a life of disarray. It's become quite commonplace to settle for far less than one is capable of. Muttering about how life is too complicated or how it's too difficult to change will do you no good. You should never accept that you can't change. Instead of being the person who simply wishes that life could be different, be the person who sees opportunity for change. Anybody who sets off to change their trajectory only does so because they know that endless good possibilities are awaiting them (Scott, 2020 & Creel, n.d.).

GOAL SETTING: MAKING IT HAPPEN

If your current method for getting things done is prompting a wide-eyed and red-faced response in you, it is definitely time to come up with a new game plan. Put constraints on how much time you will spend preparing for your day. If you stretch this out too long, your productivity tanks along with your pride in a day's work. Avoid making mental notes of what you want to hammer out for the day and instead write it down so that it will free up mental space. Highlight your most urgent goals and the timeframe you would like to complete them in. By making your goals specific and realistic, you'll have a positive outlook for the day ahead (Voltolina, 2017 & Scott, 2020).

Be aware that there are some things that land on your to-do list that just aren't that important. It's not worth stressing over all the things that you didn't get to complete. You only have so much energy in a day, and you have to be realistic about what you can accomplish. If you try to do too much, you will end up doing low-quality work. While you don't want to have a limited mindset, you can realistically only do so much in a day. If there are people in your life expecting far too much, recognize where you would like to pull away to prioritize your most important goals (Voltolina, 2017 & Scott, 2020).

There is nothing valuable about setting such high standards for yourself that you end up maxed out like an overworked racehorse. Pacing yourself is the best way to build a sustainable routine that works for you and your high standards. It truly is just as detrimental to expect too much from yourself as it is to expect far too little. Finding a balance seems to be as difficult as trying to figure out what happened to Amelia Earhart in 1937 (History, 2020); although, I do have my theories, but I might save them for my next book. While it may seem as though there is no such thing as a balanced life, don't sell yourself short by assuming this as a fact.

Finding balance isn't easy but it doesn't have to be so impossible either. A balanced life is not the equivalent of a perfect life, but it is one that gives you room to breathe. When you make time for the most important things and you set goals that you can achieve, striking that balance won't seem so impossible. In fact, the people who do say that a balanced life is impossible probably are the most disorganized among us. Balance is within reach for those who are willing to make the changes necessary to take hold of it. Have a whatever-it-takes mindset and you'll go far. (When you get there, take a picture and send it to whoever told you a balanced life doesn't exist.)

CONCLUDING THOUGHTS

In this chapter, you learned how your surroundings affect your anxiety and stress levels. If you have a messy home and work environment, you now understand how this is contributing to the way that you are feeling, which hasn't been all rainbows and sunshine. By staying organized, you can learn to be on top of your game and conquer your anxiety and stress. Also, this chapter shows how staying organized can help you to stay on track with maintaining your new habits. Don't expect things to change overnight (a new habit takes 21 days to stick), but know that you can get to where you want to be.

3

LOOK AROUND YOU AND FREE YOURSELF FROM NEGATIVE INFLUENCE

"Don't let negative and toxic people rent space in your head. Raise the rent and kick them out."

— *ROBERT TEW*

E nvironmental stress is a wide and quite varied subject and the effects are many. According to Group (2018), "Environmental stress refers to how people or animals respond to physical, chemical and biological features of their environment" (para. 3). Humans can face environmental stressors that range from poor access to food, breathing in toxic chemicals, coping with a negative home environment, and dramatic changes in weather. Just about anything in the environment can lead to some form of stress. Take a single fly buzzing in your ear. That little nuisance can produce a negative response that still lingers even after you have successfully swatted it away and reminded it who the apex predator in your house is. The different kinds of environmental stress may surprise you but each has an impact on your life, even if you aren't consciously aware of it (Group, 2018).

ENVIRONMENTAL CALAMITY

You may hear about a flood crashing into a town miles away but you never think that it will happen to you. That is, until it does. The shock of losing your home and the familiarity that it provides is enough to send anyone (rightly) over the edge. Desperation, fear, and hopelessness set in as you seek out limited recovery options available to you. The resulting trauma of this experience can provoke disturbing nightmares, ongoing stress, and worries about the future. However, if you are only witnessing these events from a distance, it can still give way to a mild stress response. Exposure to the news can prompt anxiety about even the smallest things and leave you wondering if disaster is about to rain down (Group, 2018).

CHANGES IN WEATHER

Changes in weather can include occurrences like a drought that causes farmers to lose their crop or a winter of heavy snow that keeps you indoors like in the movie *The Shining* (although, hopefully, not to that extreme, and if you find yourself yelling, "Here's Johnny!" um, then you definitely understand weather stress). On a larger scale, fluctuating weather has a great influence on mental and physical well-being. Climate changes, like those produced by global warming, force us to react and change our behaviors. The results can be hazardous to survival and destructive to mental health (Group, 2018).

MANUFACTURED IRRITANTS AND TOXINS

Unfortunately, the luxuries of the modern world also come with the dark side of ongoing exposure to toxicities across the board. Everything from the food we consume to the products we use to wash our clothes can have a negative impact on our health. Chemicals saturate the very air we breathe, and until there is a change on a global scale, this stressor will continue to affect our health (Group, 2018).

URBAN AND RURAL TRIGGERS

This stressor is quite unique because it flies under the radar given that life in the city is so normal. Anthropogenic stressors are the result of overstimulation of nonstop noise, busy streets, overpopulated areas, and ever-present activity. If you've ever slipped off your noise-canceling headphones and have been stunned by the ambient noise pressing in on you, then you understand this stressor well. According to Group (2018), "People who live near car, aircraft, and railway noise experience higher blood sugar and diabetes, increased blood pressure, greater arterial stiffness (a contributor to heart disease), and higher levels of stress hormones" (para. 30).

THE SURROUNDING VICINITY

The objects in your physical proximity can trigger stress, even in seemingly innocent ways, such as the use of artificial lights late into the evening. While this may not seem like much of a concern, the continuous exposure puts you at risk for some health issues. For example, you may experience a drop in your melatonin levels and an interference with your body's circadian rhythms if you experience an overexposure to artificial light. How many times have you stayed up late scrolling through Twitter only to experience sleeplessness when you do try to fall into sweet slumber? Probably, if you're like me, too many times to count. Physical environment stressors can also include color and energetic vibrations. If you've ever noticed that someone wearing a bright orange shirt feels painful to look at or stepping into a certain gift shop makes you feel physically ill, these are physical environment stressors that are causing these reactions (Group, 2018).

THE NUISANCE OF BIOLOGY

Biological stress can range from allergies to viruses that invade your body. Bacteria and parasites also fall into this category and require a strong immune system to fight them off (Group, 2018). Any type of ailment that you battle is kicking your body into high gear and causing a great deal of stress in the process. Recurring illnesses can be the building blocks to an extreme physical or mental breakdown. If you've ever read up on Lyme disease, you can understand how persistent illnesses run the body down. This disease, in particular, has the power to knock the wind out of you and keep you down for months, potentially affecting your health for years afterward.

LOWERING THE IMPACT OF ENVIRONMENTAL PREDICAMENTS

Rather than shrugging your shoulders and succumbing to the environmental stressors you face, it's important to do your part.

Most of us do not have the option to live on an eco-friendly island in the middle of the Pacific Ocean (although, if you hear of any real estate for sale like that, let me know). The next best thing is to seek out ways to limit, or in some cases, eliminate the stressor.

If you live within spitting distance of a factory and you have the funds to pound a "FOR SALE" sign in your front yard, by all means, do it. If you have to stay put, grab a shovel and plant some trees and bushes to cushion against the onslaught of chemicals flying your way. This will also help to reduce the noise that sneaks in through your windows, shattering the would-be peaceful moments with Felix the cat (Group, 2018).

You can also invest in a white noise generator to induce a calmer atmosphere in your home. This may not seem like much, but it has a way of blocking out the unwanted noises and giving you the peace of mind you need.

Purchasing an air filter can help to cleanse the oxygen in your home and keep the nasty chemicals out of your lungs (maybe now you can belt out those high notes on karaoke night and beam with pride at the Outstanding Vocalist Award perched above the fireplace). To keep those lungs strong, you can also drag your trash can around the house and chuck all the products in your home that are toxic. To replace them look around for products that are organic and maintain a higher standard (Group, 2018).

To better handle stress and remain a proactive problem solver, you need to cultivate resilience. The more adaptable you are, the higher the chance you have at tackling obstacles over the long-term. By being resilient, you will find that your stress is scaled down and you can move forward. According to Group (2018), the American Psychological Association has assembled the following checklist of things that you can do to buck up your resilience for long-haul mental health:

- make good relationships a priority
- refrain from viewing a crisis or stressful incidents as fatal
- let go of what you cannot control
- establish reasonable goals and resolve to accomplish them
- move with a determined plan of action in crushing circumstances
- examine opportunities for growth after overcoming a grievance
- foster self-confidence
- hold onto a big picture view when facing a stressful situation
- believe in the desires that you yearn for and foresee them happening
- nurture your mind, get out and exercise, observe your emotions, and address your needs (para. 58)

To aid in the process of building your resiliency, it's important to spend time with Mother Nature. While you don't have to go all granola hippie, grow out your hair, and throw peace signs around, getting outdoors *will* make you feel better. Remember when you were a kid and there was nothing better than going outside, climbing a tree, and feeling like you had escaped the world? That's the feeling I'm talking about. Take advantage of this readily available resource to reduce your stress and heighten your resilience. Some ways to infuse more nature into your life include: walking in the grass without shoes, filling your home with potted plants, going for a hike, or buying a new pet (Group, 2018).

DISMISSING NEGATIVE NANCY FROM YOUR LIFE

Understanding how the environment causes fluctuations in your stress levels is only half the battle. The people who are in your life can also put a strain on your mental health. The hardest lessons to learn are often the most life changing, like how you learned to perfectly flip a fried egg. The lesson here is that negative people need to be removed from your life if you are going to attain the level of achievement that you desire most: a life without stress or anxiety. Learning how to do this can be a struggle but it is well worth the effort put in. Holding onto negative people will only hold you back. Sometimes, you have to let people go and dearly hope that they do not fly back to you.

Why the Naysayers Will Destroy Your Viewpoint

You turn into the people who you choose to spend time with. Even though telling someone that you can no longer be friends might seem like a petty thing to do, it's not. Putting boundaries up in your life will mean the difference between being happy or allowing the quality of your life to deflate like a balloon from last year's New Year's Eve party. If your "friends" exhaust your energy reserves, it's time to drop them (Nick, 2019). You don't want negative people to influence you into having a negative outlook like them.

How the Naysayers Will Hamper Your Profession

It's highly unlikely that you can waste your time with negative people and not damage your value in the eyes of others. By associating with people who are not worth your time, individuals in your profession will be less inclined to network with you. If you wish to advance in your career, you have to learn to cut ties with certain people who will taint all that you have worked for. The positive people who you want to connect with want nothing to do with those negative people in your life. It's like having a big stain on your shirt: everyone knows it's there and gives you a wide berth just in case you spill something on them, too. Remove those negative people and you are paving the way to networking with professionals who can support you on your path to success (Nick, 2019).

Naysayers Will Not Push You Toward Your Dreams

Negative people will be the ones to discourage you from trying something ambitious. If you aim high, they will tell you to aim lower. Bringing yourself down to their level is not going to get you anywhere in life. These are the people who will insist that you be "realistic" and tell you to "get your head out of the clouds." But sometimes, the clouds are exactly where you should be. These people trample any sense of hope out of you until you settle for some version of yourself that wants nothing more than cynicism. Do not fall for the way that these individuals present themselves and instead, make room for people of character who want to support you (Doyle, n.d.).

Naysayers Will Pick Fights

These individuals don't get enough satisfaction from watching the drama on *General Hospital*, so they feel this ever-present need to play the victim and pick fights. Someone who feeds off the drama that they generate has not matured enough to deserve your time. Life is complicated enough without inviting in the unnecessary stress of listening to someone bemoan their unfortunate circumstances. (This is where you pretend that you have to catch your flight to Bermuda to join a volunteer group saving endangered species.) Make it a point to screen for these types of people and refrain from letting them into your life in the first place (Doyle, n.d.).

Naysayers Don't Have Your Back

Negative individuals don't care about making sure you're taken care of as a friend; they only seek out their own self-interest. These types of people only want what they can get from you like a tick. Once they see that there is nothing left to gain, they disappear. This is not a give-and-take friendship that you deserve to have. You want friends in your life who will help you make a greater contribution to this planet. Set this standard and you will find that negative people fall away from your life (Toney, 2019).

Deflecting Naysayers: Game Plan for Self-Preservation

Here is a game plan you can use to deflect naysayers like Shaq once batted away those basketballs:

1. Be on high alert for discussions that tend to lead to arguments. Aim to handle these areas with a peaceful stance that is also honest and direct instead. (Brenner, 2018)

2. Plan ahead if you know that you will be dealing with a difficult family member or colleague. Maybe consider ducking out early, if you can, so that you are able to limit contact with this person. (Brenner, 2018)

3. Stay neutral when a family member or coworker is

complaining about something and recognize that you cannot do anything about their attitude. It helps to also stay neutral to your emotional turmoil as well so that you are not reacting to what is being said. (Oakley, 2016)

4. In a tense situation, a very useful tactic is to simply surrender and observe the thoughts and emotions that are rushing through your body. Accept them as they are and don't try to change anything, as this will add to the struggle. The goal is always inner peace and by attaining it, you will be far less influenced by your surroundings. (Oakley, 2016)

5. Make yourself aware of the storytelling habits people use to cope. Negative people probably have stories that they have carried with them for years. On the basis of these stories, they are convinced that things are not right, nor will they ever be right. Whether real or imagined, these mental thoughts are like a thread on a spinning wheel (talk about an out-of-date analogy, I know, but think Rose from *Sleeping Beauty* and the wheel that she pricks her finger on). (Oakley, 2016)

6. Join a support group where you can discuss what is happening in your life and get the perspective you need most. Often, just being heard is all that you really need. It's an added benefit that you can also listen to others who are struggling with the same thing you are.

Knowing that you are not all alone in your struggles with toxic family members can be the biggest relief of all. (This is where your jaw drops, because there are others in the group who have family members that are just as crazy as yours!)

7. Keeping things casual can be one of the very best tools to use. If you don't get too personal then they have nothing to criticize you about. Colleagues or family will naturally reflect what you put out, and if you don't share personal details, it's likely that they won't either.

8. Spend time away from the toxic people in your life as often as you can. Schedule things that get you out into the world to meet other people (and if you're too tired this weekend, just pretend to be busy! White lies are okay here, I promise). If the toxic people in your world think that you lead a busy life, then they probably won't call you or drop by. (Clay, n.d.)

9. Don't waste your time ruminating on what the toxic people in your life said or did recently that has upset you, as this can drain you. (You might as well hook yourself up to a machine to donate plasma because it will require just as much energy, but at least this way you'll save lives.)

10. This may sound corny, but keep an open mind: If you think of the toxic people in your life as a compass for what you need to work on, it can actually benefit you in

the long run. When you come into contact with these people, what you find upsetting or hurtful will be clear to you. This conflict gives you the space to reflect on these areas of your life and work on healing them. Maybe one day, you will no longer be disturbed by these "hot spots" because they have evaporated with all the deep emotional work you have been doing. (Clay, n.d.)

DETECTING POISONOUS PEOPLE

Perhaps, there are people in your life who bother or upset you, but you can't quite put your finger on why. Well, below is a Magic 8-Ball guide to how to detect the poisonous people in your life and how to handle them.

The Angry Fatalistic Type

This person in your life walks around as if they have a weight they are dragging around. In a literal sense, they do because of the burdensome energy that they bring everywhere. They only see what is wrong with life and not the things that are going well. These people look for reasons to be unhappy and make no effort to smile. Imagine Darth Vader on a good day. If you cannot escape these individuals because you work together or they are family, there are ways to keep them from draining you (Locke, n.d.).

Here are tips for dealing with this type of person:

- Limit your interactions with them and don't get personal.
- Be clear about how you will not be present with their negativity.
- Find ways to bring positivity into your life, anything that can switch your mindset.
- Refuse to be influenced by negativity and remain strong in your positive outlook.
- When conflict arises with them, step away and don't look back.
- Reframe the negative person in your life as a chance to expand your strength.
- Focus your attention on the people who matter most to you. (Hurst, n.d.)

The Belittling Type

This person will regularly take note of everything that is wrong about a situation, rub it in your face, and make you look like you just lost a pie-eating contest. From the way that you file papers to the way that you dress, everything is up for criticism. This person lives to judge you and may even relish in the experience. Putting you down gives them a sense of power over you and builds up their ego. There are ways that you can cope with these types and prevent them from tainting your perspective (Hurst, n.d.).

Here's how to deal with belittlers (not to be confused with bedwetters, totally different thing, although, there may be some overlap, who's to say):

- Try to see things objectively and don't take their words to heart.
- See where their criticism can help you become an improved version of yourself.
- Be impartial when lethal criticism is tossed at you, and it will bounce right off you.
- Follow the motto: you have the right to remain silent. (This isn't just a phrase for cops during arrest; it's a tool for you to regain your power and find your center.)
- Don't be too hard on yourself because no one is flawless, and perfection is an illusion.
- Take the bird's eye view of the situation, and you'll discover that your feelings don't get hurt so easily by bedwetters, I mean, belittlers.
- Find reasons to smile because positivity is your strongest weapon against this person. (Hurst, n.d.)

The Needy Type

This person is very much like a child, and you have to think of them like one. This mainly involves strategizing so that the ball is in your court and never in theirs (think of Shaq again). If you give this individual free reign, they will drag you wherever they want to take you. It's very important that you have a game plan ready at all times so that your schedule is never being tossed into the gutter by them. Your time is too valuable to be wasted on someone who never knew how to find the willpower to gain maturity and interpersonal awareness (Hurst, n.d.).

To manage the needy ones in your life, here are some tips:

- If you are dealing with them on a personal level, always know the outcome they are looking for when they ask you to sit down and talk.
- If you are dealing with this person at work, try to keep things professional, and if they go on a tangent in a meeting, direct the conversation back on track.
- Set limits on how you will communicate with this individual and make it clear what you find unacceptable.
- If you find it feasible, spend time with this person in a larger group so that you have the option to redirect your attention to someone else instead. (Hurst, n.d.)

The Daily Misfortune Type

For this individual, life is always unfair. Think Debbie Downer times the power of a million burning suns. These people think that there is someone else responsible for the problems they are dealing with. They don't want to accept that they are the ones responsible for the quality of their lives. They will always be searching for someone to bail them out of the pain that life offers everyone. Sometimes, difficult circumstances are how we grow and become the best version of ourselves, but try telling them that. These people would rather stay where they are at because it's easier, and it gives them permission to fixate on their problems (Hurst, n.d.).

For dealing with the drag that is a daily misfortune type, try the below advice:

- If this person won't take responsibility, even when you encourage them to do so, then stop giving them advice altogether.
- If they choose to remain where they are, it's not your job to toss them a lifeline; instead, let them learn on their own time.
- If you have to discuss something with them, diffuse their victim mentality by stating that your feedback is not meant to bring them down but to resolve the matter and move forward.

- When this person is engaged in a downward spiral, make it a point to change the subject or excuse yourself because your sympathy will only reinforce that their lives are bad enough to sink even deeper.

- Even when this individual gets what they want, they will still remain dissatisfied because of what they don't have. Don't waste your time trying to make them happy, because they will only magnify what is absent. (Hurst, n.d.)

The Egotistical Type

This individual is always asking but never giving back to you. They don't invest in your friendship, but instead dump their baggage on you like you're the doorman in a high-class apartment building. This person may have grown up believing that life is all about them, and this feeling persists in adulthood. These individuals have a veil over their eyes, and they firmly believe that they are entitled to everything they want. This means that, at your expense, they will seize what they can get and disregard how their poor choice leaves you to clean up the mess (Hurst, n.d.).

The ego is a tough one to crack, but you can try the following:

- Refuse to be a doormat, because you expect everyone to treat you with respect.

- Reinforce your boundaries and make them durable like a steel building. Point out that they won't be crossing these boundaries, and you'll make sure of it.

- If you need to, bring on extra support when you aren't getting the results you want. Force this person to see that if their behavior continues, they will have to endure the consequences.

- If you see that this individual is manipulative, be honest with them that you see right through their tactics, and you won't be playing along.

- Recognize that this person will get what is coming to them, even if it seems like they get away with everything (karma is a b—, well you know the saying). They will eventually have to deal with the repercussions. Remember that it's not your role to teach them. Sometimes, all you can do is sit back and watch them self-destruct. (Hurst, n.d.)

The Static Type

This person will continue to make the same mistakes over and over and over—well, you get the picture. They will also fail to grow beyond them. They will disappoint you. Some stagnant types put in the effort to make a living, but they have plateaued. They have no interest in putting in more than what is expected of them, and they will probably live out their days this way. There is another stagnant type that is worse, as this person puts no effort in whatsoever. This individual simply does not care and is happy mooching off of others to get by (Hurst, n.d.).

Buffering, buffering, buffering—here's how to manage the static people in your life:

- Do not feed the stagnancy by accepting the behavior, but instead make it clear that you are dissatisfied.
- Even though you've expressed your concerns, don't expect this person to change. Expectations will lead to more disappointment, which is a true drain on your energy.
- You know that this person can do better, but until they see the truth, they will continue in their ways. Some people need to go through self-inflicted hardship before they can see the light. Only then, when they have had enough, will they change the course of their lives.
- Do not invest your time ruminating on this person and their decisions. Put up a barrier so that you are not rushing to go save a sinking ship, so to speak. You have to understand that this individual has not yet gotten the memo that life is sending their way. Your only job is to accept what you cannot change. (Hurst, n.d.)

Sometimes it's not feasible to remove these types of people from your life. Even if you leave your job because of one toxic person, you can end up in a job with three more. You might have an unhealthy family member that is woven deeply into the fabric of your clan. To no longer associate with them is possibly cutting off the rest of your family as well. Your best option then would be to look for ways to guard yourself against these negative influences. Just because someone is in your life doesn't mean that they can have their way with your mind. You decide how you respond to every situation. Don't give anyone the satisfaction of making that choice for you.

Seek Out Positive Individuals and Master Their Ways

Positive people are everywhere, which is why there is no reason to hang out with negative people. If you make an effort to search for these influences and spend enough time with them, you will discover that you, too, can be a positive person.

Noticing the rays of sunshine that fill this planet can be quite difficult at times, especially when it means that you have to step out into left field (stepping on to right field will just lead you to first base, and trust me, that'll only help you out in the dating game). Finding good friends isn't a piece of cake, but it's the best slice that life has to offer.

Here are some qualities you want to look for when searching for that best bud to fill the gap in your life:

- Positive friends will be there when you need them and will lift you up when you feel bogged down.

- Respect is their way of life, and they will honor you and all that you hope to accomplish.

- They are doing amazing things in the world and want the same exact results for you. They will always give you advice without overstepping your boundaries.

- They will look for reasons to laugh and will often laugh at themselves. They will smile even in hard times because they know life is too short to be upset by the little things that try to knock them down.

- They are honest about how they feel and will always tell you if something in your friendship needs to be addressed. Just because they are positive, doesn't mean they are willing to sugarcoat the hard things in life.

- They are accepting of their shortcomings, as well as yours, and they know that there is always work to be done to improve. They know when they've messed up and are willing to step up to apologize for their wrongdoings.

- They are steadfast in their determination to make a better life for themselves and others. They know better than to give up when times get tough, and instead, they push even harder to reach the victory line.

- They have a strong belief that life is good, in spite of all the bad things that happen in the world. Even in the worst situations, they are looking for the spark that signifies that the human spirit can overcome absolutely anything. This is what keeps them going, because even when they can't see that spark, they know it's there. (Staff Author, 2020 & Power of Positivity, n.d.)

Establishing Rapport With the Right People

Once you find the good ones, you'll want to work at keeping them in your life. The better you are at communicating, the more likely you will attract quality people into your life. People of high standards want to see that you can be attentive, regard others with consideration, be supportive, and tell the truth. By imparting your knowledge and your finances to things that matter to you, there is a good chance you will find more generosity slipping into your life. This enthusiasm will invite more courteous people to drop into your life. You'll see how kindness ripples out only to find its way back to you (Team Tony, n.d., Dienstman, A.M., 2018 & Martinez, N. 2020).

FINAL REMARKS

This chapter covered the many ways that the environment can take a toll on your body and on your ability to cope with life's stressors. The environment is often not thought of as a cause of stress and anxiety, but the role that it plays is undeniable. You learned about the facts that prove that the environment influences every part of our lives, even the things that can appear to be harmless. You learned ways that you can lessen the impact that the environment has on your body. There are ways to replenish your body and create barriers so that you live relatively free of the harsh toxins that can damage your mental, emotional, and physical health.

You also learned about toxic people and how to properly deal with them to decrease the stress and anxiety that filters into your life. Filling your life with positive people is the best thing you can do to not only improve your social circle, but better manage the busy life that you lead. You don't have time to waste on negative people, so cut out the ones that you can and leave room for the best that life has to offer you. It may be hard, but it's much better to make a painful decision now than have to deal with the consequences of avoiding it.

4

THE NEW CONFIDENT YOU

"If you hear a voice within you say 'you cannot paint,' then by all means paint, and that voice will be silenced."

— *VINCENT VAN GOGH*

S tress and anxiety can cause a decline in self-esteem and confidence that affects the way we function, which, in turn, causes more stress and anxiety. This is a cyclical process, and the cause and effect is not so straightforward. It's kind of like those daredevils who used to ride motorbikes in a metal cage: round and round they went, picking up speed as they defied gravity. Well, in this metaphor, your stress is the daredevil, your anxiety is the motorbike, and you're the metal cage (with very low self-esteem). A perfect system of contained chaos.

If that's not bad enough, low self-esteem can make you believe that you are useless and unable to rise to any challenge. So, rather than falling short, you might not even try at all, because at least that way you can retain your current view of yourself.

On the other hand, stress laid on thick can cause someone who is normally confident to lose their grip. Suddenly, a bright individual only has the endurance to make a bowl of cereal and slump on the couch, falling asleep to reruns of *Saved by the Bell.*

In either case, it is the person's vantage point that forges this response to retreat in the face of perceived danger. Stress colors their perception and makes it impossible for them to take on the hurdles that are before them. This heavy-laden perception is what keeps those with chronic low self-esteem on the mental track that they are weak and defenseless when adversity is looming over them. This is the reason why it's so crucial to develop one's self-esteem.

High self-esteem will support you as you wade through challenges and aid you in seeing things through. Increased confidence is one of the best ways to decrease stress levels because it acts like a shield.

CONFIDENCE BREAKTHROUGHS: TECHNIQUES AND EXERCISES

The following sections will allow you to safely explore how you can build your confidence and become the He-Man (or woman) you know you are deep down.

Running Toward Fear

This technique is about as straightforward as they come. In order to overcome your fear, you need to face the beast that you have been running from (unless the thing you fear is an actual grizzly bear, in that case, run like you are training for a marathon). The things that you will be exposing yourself to are not actually life-threatening, but there is a stress response in your body that makes you react otherwise. By facing these fears, you will come to see that they are not nearly as scary as you thought (Anxiety Canada, n.d.).

Case Study:

Kelly has been refusing to go to the zoo with her family every year because she is terrified of the alligators. She always imagines one of them leaping over the enclosure and biting off her arm. She can vividly see the frantic crowd scatter and the paramedic crew arriving to save her mangled upper limb. In her vision of the scene, she pictures being carted off to the hospital only to learn that her arm cannot be reconstructed, and she is filled with regret that she ever so much as heard the words "Zany's Magical Performance Featuring Live Alligators."

The process of practicing fear exposure can be quite overwhelming, so it's important to break it down. Things are only complicated when you engage in the behaviors of over-thinking and worrying. Grab a notebook and follow the steps in the next section ensure that you face your fears head on.

Guidelines for Dealing With Fear:

1. Reflect on the things that you are afraid of and write them all down. These could be events, locations, or items that you are afraid of.

2. Classify each fear based on the degree to which you have an emotional reaction. Beside each fear you can simply mark off where it falls on the scale from zero (fear is absent) to ten (fear is intense).

3. Circle the fears that are on the low end of the scale and highlight the ones that bring out the strongest fear response.

4. Begin by facing the fears that are on the lower end of the spectrum. The more you make it a point to expose yourself to these fears, the less you will have a fearful reaction. Engage with each fear until you see a dramatic drop in your anxiety.

5. Once you have dealt with the circled fears, it's time to

face the ones that you highlighted. Take this process a little slower than you did with the first set of fears. You will need time to adjust as your fear slowly evaporates. Eventually, you will see that these fears will become commonplace and that you can train your body to react differently.

6. After you have ticked off everything on your list (hold for applause), all you need to do is continue dealing with these fears. The more time you invest into this, the more confident you will feel facing these fears.

7. Over time, you can lessen the exposure since you no longer fear these activities. However, it is possible to regress back to old fears that you've worked so hard to remove from your life. Make it a point to check back in with these fears and see how you respond when you open yourself up to them again. (Anxiety Canada, n.d.)

Psychological Vulnerability

The goal of this exercise is to face flashbacks and thoughts that still linger in your mind after the event has passed. This exercise has a far different approach from the previous one but can be just as overwhelming. Take breaks when you need to. But it's important to work through traumatic events and the feelings they cause and to also dispel the power that they have over you. This exercise may cause some distress, so have a plan in place of what you would like to do afterward to support yourself (Anxiety Canada, n.d.).

Case Study:

A few years ago, Jared's house caught on fire. The entire home was nearly engulfed in flames before he awoke. There was a fireman who smashed open his window and pulled him out, and without his bravery, Jared probably wouldn't be alive today. This event was especially difficult because he lost his dog in this fire. For Jared, Levi was more than just a dog; he was his best friend. Homes can be rebuilt, but companions can never be replaced.

Guidelines for Psychological Vulnerability:

1. Pick out a memory that is hanging in your mind like a deadweight.
2. Choose an allotted time frame to do this exercise. Set an alarm for thirty to sixty minutes from now.
3. Write out the details of this memory as if it is happening in this moment.
4. Include what you can recall but don't be concerned if some of the nuances fall between the cracks.
5. Once you reach the end of the memory, make a note of how stressful or upsetting this was to you on a scale of zero to ten.
6. By the end of the exercise, the outcome is for you to discharge the pent-up emotions surrounding this event.

Like air releasing from a valve, the hope is that you would feel a great sense of relief.

7. When you feel ready, the next part of this exercise will ask you to read over what you have written. Set an alarm again and have a plan in place of what you will do afterward to nurture yourself. Reading the memories aloud may help you to process them a little easier. As you read, make a note again of how you feel on the same scale of zero to ten.

8. Repeat the same process from the previous step. The idea here is that this memory will gradually lose its hold on you. You will find that your stress rating will drop each time you read your words out loud.

9. The objective is not to dismiss what happened to you, but to take back your emotional freedom. The less power this event has over you as you move forward in life, the greater the chance you have to experience all that life has to offer. Life tends to have more vivid colors and carry a stronger purpose when it is not fogged up by painful memories of the past.

10. When you are able to come back to this exercise, rewrite the memory and include more specifics. These details could be thoughts you may not have recalled the first time around. You may even find yourself including the five senses as you write.

11. If you feel that you are prepared to share this memory,

seek out someone that you can confide in. Read it out loud to them or if you feel more comfortable, have them read it. Sharing your painful experiences can pave the way to stronger bonds and even more profound healing experiences. (Anxiety Canada, n.d.)

Detaching From The Easy Way Out

People who find themselves feeling overly anxious engage in behaviors that decrease some of the anxiety in the short-term. These behaviors are like a crutch as they don't offer any long-term results to resolve the issue and only serve to reinforce the existing anxiety. These behaviors are exhausting to the one who practices them and to everyone around them. The best solution is to find ways to lessen and eventually eliminate these quick fixes from interfering with daily life (Anxiety Canada, n.d.).

Case Study:

Nora often worries about her mother because she insists on living alone. Since her mother is in her late eighties, she is at risk for all kinds of health ailments. Nora calls her mother every few hours to make sure she hasn't fallen due to the fact that she has to use a walker to get around. Nora's husband, Jim, is quite frustrated because he feels that her quick fixes are interfering with their relationship. She will often get up in the middle of dinner "just to make sure that mom is okay." Jim feels that if she doesn't get a handle on her behavior, it will only continue to get worse as the years pass by.

Guidelines for Detaching From the Easy Way Out:

1. Write down all the behaviors that you engage in when you are looking for an easy way out.

2. Beside each behavior, write down a more appropriate action and then rate how anxious it would make you feel to engage in this behavior instead.

3. One of the best things you can do is suspend the impulse to carry out the behavior. Find an activity that you can do to distract yourself. If you feel that your impulse is reduced, you are already making progress.

4. Set up reminders around your home to keep the new behaviors at the forefront of your mind.

5. Take time to reflect at the end of each day or each week and journal about your breakthroughs. Write about what you still need to change and where you are still struggling to make headway.

6. Confide with the people in your life and ask them to support you as you are trying to reduce the impact that these quick fixes have on your life.

7. Sit down and review the new behaviors that you laid out in step 2. If you feel differently, journal about what has changed and what has remained the same. (Anxiety Canada, n.d.).

Challenge Your Anguish

People who worry excessively find uncertainty to be intolerable. Worry is how they cope with uncertain times, regardless of the situation being of actual concern. Embracing not knowing what the future will bring is a much better way to cope. Worrying has a phony way of tripping the brain into thinking that something is being accomplished by pondering all the things that could happen. Being comfortable with uncertainty is not only a better way to cope but it's far more practical. Life is filled with unpredictable outcomes. There are ways to establish acceptance around uncertainty, which will make everyday life smoother and spare you the heartache of worry (Anxiety Canada, n.d.).

Case Study:

Logan is often worrying about his medical school goals. The competition is fierce and earning his undergraduate degree is going to be incredibly strenuous. He often worries if his grades will be good enough to get into a solid graduate program, much less find a job as a surgeon. His dream is to go overseas with the nonprofit Doctors Without Borders, but he has years ahead of him before he can even apply. His worst fear is never reaching his potential, and it plagues his thoughts throughout the day.

Guidelines for Challenging Your Anguish:

1. If there are worried thoughts popping up in your head

about today's tasks or plans, move through them as best you can. Sometimes, all you need is the satisfaction of knowing that something is completed to lessen your troubled thoughts.

2. Give your attention over to things that you can personally regulate. Even if you feel like your whole life is spinning out of control, exerting the power to influence certain tasks can be a major stress reliever.

3. If your worries seem to be taking over, you have to force yourself to get physically moving. Movement shifts your thoughts and makes you more proactive about what you can do to change your situation. It doesn't matter if you decide to go to a yoga class or clean your garage, any movement is better than being at a standstill. Make it a point to get out into the world rather than being closed off in your mind at all times.

4. The worst of your problems can often lie between your earlobes. If you change the way you think, you've already begun the process of changing your life. Write out everything you are afraid of that might happen this week. Then write out the most desirable outcome and picture this happening in place of your worst fears. This mental reassurance can be like a tonic for your fears.

5. Another practice that can be helpful is writing out a storyline about your fear happening in the near future. By writing this story out, you are confronting your

fears and experiencing them in the present moment. Rather than having an ill-defined worry floating around in your head, you now have a precise account of what you are afraid of. Identifying specific worries means that you have something to work with, and it is more plausible for you to tackle it. This is akin to finally getting a diagnosis and undergoing treatment versus wondering why you have a severe ongoing migraine with no end in sight. If you are able to write in such a way that brings out your true feelings about this possible outcome, it will help to reduce your anxiety. (Anxiety Canada, n.d.)

Constructive Dialogue Within

Your internal dialogue can be a huge drain on your confidence if you don't make an effort to manage it. It's important to be aware of how your inner voice processes situations and how those thoughts are directed back to you. If the way you communicate with yourself is pessimistic, it may be the cause of much of your stress. Viewing the circumstances of your life as bad and blaming yourself for the things that go wrong can often be a component of this negativity. Life can be problematic, and it is through resolving these problems that we learn how to be better people. If you see these problems as walls materializing to obstruct your happiness, negative self-talk will likely consume your life (Anxiety Canada, n.d.).

Case Study:

Ava grew up with an auditory disability because of repeated ear infections that were not properly treated. She suffers from an auditory processing disorder and finds daily life to be quite difficult. Her disability isn't obvious since she isn't required to wear hearing aids. Even though she can hear just fine, she processes what she's hearing with great difficulty. Ava's self-talk is pretty harsh at times because she is forced to work much harder than her coworkers. No matter how hard she works, it never feels like it's enough.

Guidelines for Constructive Dialogue:

1. It can seem as though your internal dialogue is "normal" but in reality it is quite degrading. It's crucial to build awareness around your self-talk so that you can put an end to the negativity. Start with writing down negative self-talk when it pops into your mind. Seeing the words on paper can be a wake-up call in and of itself.

2. When negativity begins to creep in, stop it before it gets a hold on you. Explore why you are feeling the need to put yourself down and find something that you are doing right. Even if you made a mistake, there is something that you did today that you can feel proud of.

3. Watering down the intensity of the words that you choose when you are upset can help to diffuse the

situation you are dealing with. Using kind and positive words can decrease the chances that you will succumb to negativity.

4. Flip a negative situation around in your mind when something goes wrong. Maybe what you are perceiving to be wrong is just different than what you expected. It's entirely possible that this inconvenience can lead to something good. Even if it feels like you are digging for buried treasure, there will be something good that comes out of it. Usually, the good that you discover is simply a life lesson (I know that might seem cringe-worthy, but everyone needs these wisdom nuggets).

5. Transitioning your fixed mindset statements into growth mindset questions is a genius way to reverse your self-talk. Fixed mindset statements involve saying things like: "This is never going to work" or "Things like this always happen to me." Growth mindset questions, however, are inquiries such as: "What are some better ways to solve this?" or "What have I learned from this experience?" The fixed mindset keeps you stuck right where you are and the growth mindset helps you to move out of the rut. (Anxiety Canada, n.d.)

Authoritative Posture

The way that you *carry* yourself affects the way that you *feel* about yourself. There are two hormones in particular that change when you utilize the authoritative posture technique: testosterone and cortisol. By taking an authoritative posture, you can reduce stress and transform the way you think about yourself. You can become a more confident and able-bodied version of yourself, so get ready to sign up for Toastmasters, because this is your moment to shine like never before (Clear, n.d.).

Case Study:

Wyatt finds himself on the verge of a panic attack every time his boss asks him to lead the quarterly meetings. His boss seems to like what he has to say (although he's not sure why because he does nothing but panic and sweat the entire time). Even though Wyatt is confident about finance management, he's not as confident when it comes to public speaking. With all eyes on him and nothing but a PowerPoint to guide the way, Wyatt feels that he would much rather be head of the luncheon committee raising funds for the local library (just saying, kids don't read enough these days).

Guidelines for Finding Your Authoritative Posture:

1. This technique involves power poses. There are a number of poses that you can do, but starting with one is best. Begin by standing tall with your feet facing forward. Set a timer for two minutes and put your hands on your hips. Drop your shoulders as you bring your chin level with the ground. Stand tall and observe

how you feel. Notice the subtle changes that course through your body. When the timer goes off, you're all finished.

2. If you make this practice a part of your morning routine, you can remain confident throughout the rest of the day. It's also best to do this technique at home and in private so that you don't get weird looks from your coworkers.

3. If you do this practice every day, you'll start to notice changes in the way that you handle challenges. You might even realize that your stress and anxiety have dropped off to an all-time low. As you go about your day, keep in mind that it's essential that you maintain a strong posture to keep those testosterone levels up.

4. Be flexible with this practice and incorporate other strategies that work well for you. There is no "one way" of approaching a morning routine, and you might even find that switching it up and trying different poses can produce different results that you didn't anticipate. (Clear, n.d.)

The Bridge Bounded by Social Anxiety and Stress

Anyone who deals with social anxiety knows that it's a tough cookie (it doesn't come with any chocolate chips, either, talk about a double whammy). Whenever you are expecting to enter a communal situation, social anxiety can show up like an unwanted visitor. Dopamine and adrenaline can create lasting feelings of apprehension, tension, and excitement. When you're distracted by the alarming frenzy elation and dread, it can be difficult to listen and respond appropriately. Situations like these are made worse when you have to answer vague questions about what you've been up to lately (Roberts, September 13).

Case Study:

Sarah has been invited to a birthday party for a friend of a friend. Although she does okay in smaller social settings, just thinking about big parties makes her want to puke her guts out. She doesn't want to go, but her friend really wants her to. At the party, Sarah immediately is overwhelmed. She tries to talk to other people, but she is sweating too much and can't find the right words. Sure that no one likes her or wants her there, she retreats to the bathroom and doesn't come out until her friend finds her, and they go home. Sarah is embarrassed and angry at herself.

Exercises and Techniques to Overcome Social Anxiety:

1. For starters, remind yourself that you belong in this social setting. No matter how anxious you feel, there is a place for you here among this crowd. Try not to overthink how others are perceiving you and focus on evidence that you belong.

2. Look around and see people with whom you relate, even if there are no familiar faces. There will be characteristics that stand out about certain people, and you will no doubt have some common interests.

3. When you feel at a loss for words, ask questions. This shows others that you take an interest in what they have to say. Plus, it makes you come across as intelligent by coming up with a thoughtful question. When the person responds, this is your chance to breathe (in a not-so-obvious way, of course, otherwise they will think you're ready to make a mad dash for the exit). As this person is talking, you will have the chance to observe, listen, and come up with more questions and thoughtful responses.

4. Getting a handle on your emotions is vital if you are going to overcome your social anxiety. Something that can make you feel a whole lot better is a simple smile. Not only will it make you feel better, but it will make those around you relax, too. It's entirely possible that the person you are talking to is anxious as well. When you smile, you let them know that you enjoy their company and that you appreciate what they have to say. They will pick up on this and prolong the conversation, easing your social anxiety in the process.

5. When you are approaching a scene that kindles your social anxiety, you'll start breathing heavier. To reduce

this reaction, practice the below breathing technique in private. This technique is very similar to a meditation practice and will naturally overlap. (Roberts, September 13, & This Way Up, n.d.)

Peaceful Breathing Technique:

- Begin by sitting down and breathing through your nostrils.
- Do this for a few minutes. Just feel your breath moving in and out.
- Bring your attention down to your lower abdomen and allow this space to control your breathing.
- Take a breath in, hold the air, and then let it out. Repeat this for roughly five minutes.
- Afterward, breathe naturally for sixty seconds. Notice if there is a change in the way that you are breathing.
- Practice this technique throughout the day when you have spare time, two to four times a day is preferable.
- When you are in social situations and feel anxious, you use this technique in a discreet manner to get the same results. (This Way Up, n.d.)

Additional Suggestions to Scale Down Social Anxiety:

1. Keep an eye out for social situations that make you

uneasy. Be open to opportunities that you would normally turn away from and recognize these as experiences that can help you defeat your social anxiety.

2. Seek out resources that can help support you with improving your mental health. Don't be ashamed of sitting down and talking to a therapist.

3. Brainstorm ways that you can upgrade your fitness regimen. Start with exercises that you enjoy doing and gradually move toward more difficult physical training.

4. Write out some benchmarks you want to meet regarding your anxiety. Include other goals that are important to your happiness and sense of accomplishment. Setting up small steps that you can take every week will keep you from holding yourself back.

5. Find ways to reward yourself. Having things to look forward to will give you increased motivation to check goals off your list. This strength will carry over to social situations as you learn that you really can accomplish anything you set out to do.

6. Educate yourself about social anxiety and be aware of what exactly you need to function well. If you need to communicate some things to the people in your life, do so. It's important to stand up for yourself, even with those who you love.

7. Give yourself a reasonable amount of time to be alone

and refresh your energy reserves. Alone time is extremely beneficial for meeting your self-care needs. Make sure that you aren't spending too much time alone since this can lead to confinement.

8. Let go of the idea that you must be perfect in order to have a good and successful life. You are not being judged by others as often as you think, and you don't have to live as if you are. Your imperfections make you human and relatable, and people will appreciate being able to see the real you.

9. Read a memoir about someone who has lived with social anxiety and overcame it. You will probably see bits and pieces of yourself in the author. You will notice the ways that they pushed through and found happiness in spite of their battles with socializing. You never know how another person's story can shift your own.

10. Travel to a new place and explore a different way of life. The most seasoned travelers will say that you learn more about yourself by taking a trip than you ever will sitting in a classroom. You will encounter challenges, uncertainty, and desserts that you didn't even know existed, like deep-fried Mars bars, which I hear are a delicacy in some parts. (Cunic, 2020)

CLOSING REFLECTIONS

This chapter covered the ways that you can overcome stress and anxiety with confidence. You discovered that it's possible to break cycles that keep you feeling down and disconnected from your true self. You also learned more about social anxiety and the role that it has in raising your stress levels. The many exercises and techniques in this chapter will help you build your confidence so that you can live a life that is free from stress, worry, and anxiety. You are now ready to move past the things that are holding you back. You got this!

5

THE POWER OF POSITIVE THOUGHTS

"The positive thinker sees the invisible, feels the intangible, and achieves the impossible."

— *WINSTON CHURCHILL*

Positive thinking has more to do with the attitude in which you handle undesirable circumstances rather than upholding a never-ending euphoria about life (which sounds exhausting, I must admit). No, you don't have to be a rah-rah cheerleader all the time to be a positive thinker; you just have to create a positive feedback loop of thoughts that propel you forward. This positivity, in turn, helps you complete tasks, meet goals, and handle tough situations without an influx of worry and stress.

Your outlook on life is a direct result of the self-talk that was mentioned in the last chapter. The things that you tell yourself and the thoughts you have about a situation will correlate with the actions that you follow. Thinking about a situation in a negative way and telling yourself you are incapable of success, inevitably, leads to failure. Positive thoughts, on the other hand, are like the Elixir to Induce Euphoria from *Harry Potter*: They make you feel like you can do anything.

Optimistic thinking can also help you cope with stress, improve your mental performance, and decrease depression. Physically, positive thinking can help with heart health and help you bounce back quicker from physical ailments.

Negative thinking, however, brings on detrimental behaviors. It makes you focus only on your perceived flaws, the negatives of any situation, and how bad things are. This self-critical lens then prevents you from achieving self-growth, seeing the obvious solutions, and taking chances to transform your personal circumstances. It's a bit like wandering around aimlessly in a fog and then finding a haunted house on a hill, and we all know what happens once you enter that house (ghosts, my friends, scary ghosts are what happen).

With positive thinking, you will see that things tend to flow more naturally as you are better equipped to handle stress. You will be more conscious of your choices, and therefore, find yourself leaning toward healthier choices. Since you will be making better decisions overall and handling problems well from the start, you won't need coping mechanisms that hold you back. You will also find yourself associating with other positive individuals, which will lead to a richer life.

To enact positive thinking, all you need to do is change your thought patterns. For example:

- Instead of thinking "I can't handle this," tell yourself "I know I can do this."
- Instead of thinking "That's impossible," tell yourself "Let's make it happen."
- Instead of thinking "There's nothing I can do about it," tell yourself "It is within my power to change."
- Instead of thinking "That's way too much work," tell yourself "I know I will grow from this."

Here are some other ways you can create a positive mindset as well:

1. When you find yourself in a particularly bad mood, take some time to write out what you're telling yourself. Find the connection point between an emotional

incident and your thoughts that surround it. Reflect on this self-talk and if it is an ongoing or rare occurrence. You want to be cognizant of the mental conversations that you are having with yourself throughout the day.

2. Become aware of where cognitive biases are rising up when you run into a challenge. These distortions throw blanket statements over situations and don't effectively deal with the problem at hand. Some examples of these biases include: pulling out rash conclusions from daily struggles, all or nothing labels, or taking things personally.

3. Make an effort to look for positive friends, and you will see how much easier it is to be positive yourself. You will quite often mirror the people who you spend time with, so it's crucial that you pick and choose who is best for your growth.

4. Replace your negative talk with useful responses that help you to move forward and accomplish a task. It's important to acknowledge how you feel while also addressing the logical solution.

5. Think about what you dream of most when you picture the future. Then, write down some affirmations that you can say every morning to start your day. Focus on the emotions that you want to evoke and make them as simple and clear as possible. Write your affirmations in the present tense to reinforce that you already have

what you want (as opposed to it being a speck far off in the distant future). Make some time in the evening and read the affirmations aloud before you go to sleep.

TECHNIQUES FOR ENACTING POSITIVE THINKING

The train to positivity doesn't only stop at a positive mindset. Below, you can explore more ways to enact a positive feedback loop and become the heavyweight champ of positivity.

Rethink Approach

This method is all about harnessing your imagination in order to reframe a situation. To do this, paint a mental picture of the situation in a positive light. Then, imagine all the good things that will follow or what you can learn about yourself through the situation. This storytelling technique is a creative way to lighten your mood and drop your stress levels by rethinking and reassessing just how bad things are (or aren't).

Looping Back Around

For one reason or another, it can be quite difficult to take the time to examine what you're thinking when an unfortunate circumstance lands in your lap. In looping back around, you want to make a quick note of your feelings so that you can return to them later. When you are able to sit down with these feelings and thoughts, you can ask yourself: Where did these feelings show up as sensations in my body? Why did they show up? What do I think would happen if I didn't feel this way? Are there ways I can feel differently in a similar situation?

The goal of this exercise is to help you understand why you handpicked these thoughts and encourages you to set them aside and choose new ones.

Contemplative Awareness

Meditation is a multi-purpose activity, as it benefits the mind, body, and soul. Meditation often asks practitioners to guide their focus to the oxygen moving in and out of the body. The other option here is to guide your focus to the mantra, or the phrase that is being repeated as the theme of the practice. Meditation can help you practice the art of letting go of negative feelings.

When problems arise, you can use these meditation tools in daily life. Bringing your attention away from the problem and instead to your breath or mantra is incredibly healing and liberating.

The Advantage Attitude

This concept connects to the growth mindset that was discussed in the previous chapter. Here, you want to train yourself to see endless, positive outcomes, no matter if the actual outcome is good or bad. This way, if something isn't turning out exactly the way you hoped, you know that this will benefit you or someone else along the way. You are able to remain more optimistic with this mindset, as you see the advantage in every outcome.

Offering Empathy Toward Yourself

By learning to see yourself with eyes of compassion, as you would with any other human, you can generate more positive emotions. Find small acts of kindness that bring a smile to your face and warm your heart. For daily practices, you can employ things like reading uplifting words at sunrise, and at sunset, find a gratitude practice that ends the day on a positive note. All of this serves as a way to offer yourself bits of empathy and kindness, reminding you that you deserve it. By keeping up with your empathy practice, you will find that your mentality does not break down nearly as much.

STAMP OUT PESSIMISTIC THINKING

While it's important to cultivate positivity like a little seedling in need of tender care (shout out to the gardeners out there!), you also need to stamp out pessimistic thinking like the weed it is.

News Hangover

While it is important to stay informed about world events, you may want to reconsider flipping on the news when you are feeling particularly negative. Daily news reports compile the worst events that are happening and then send them your way. If you think about it, this is just as bad as having a friend arrive at your home only to sink into a chair and describe all the horrible things that happened to them throughout their entire life. Before you grab your camera to snap a picture of your flatscreen and sell it to the first bidder on eBay, however, consider that you simply need to set some boundaries. Reducing your watch time can have a dramatic effect on your mood.

Write It Out

Writing down the negative thoughts that are swirling around in your head can have a huge impact on your life. This practice not only helps you become more conscious of why you find yourself in a bad mood, but it can help slow the negative thoughts down. This gives you the space to regain your balance, and it gives you permission to feel the negativity and acknowledge what you can do to change the tides. You might even find that this exercise aids you in feeling more positive because the thoughts are no longer holding you captive. Like a prisoner of war being released from the confines of four walls, you are no longer held hostage by these repetitive thoughts.

Be One With Nature

Being in nature is a great way to diminish negative thoughts. When you are surrounded by trees, chirping birds, and nothing artificial, you give your body and mind permission to press the reset button. Sometimes, all you need is to distance yourself from a problem by getting outside, and then you will see that the issue at hand was those jam-packed negative thought loops.

Use the Negative for Good

Negative feelings don't have to be a bad thing. Keep in mind that there is no way to destroy all negative thoughts and remain positive 24/7. This is not only an unrealistic goal but it's unhealthy. Negative thoughts can help you out when you are being mistreated or when something clashes with your value system. Sometimes, negative emotions help you to see where you need to work on yourself.

Affirm Yourself

To remove pessimism, you must affirm the positive. Using affirmations can help to reinforce what it is that you want and empower you to go out and seize the day. Negativity can show up when you fall for the belief that you can't have what you want. It's all too easy to walk right into this trap when you compare yourself to others who seem to have it all. Remember you aren't unlucky because you don't have an inground pool in your backyard and a butler named Jeeves serving you fresh wine and cheese (boy, ain't that the dream). Affirm that you have a great life with wonderful opportunities. Believe that you can have what you want, and there is no such thing as aiming too high.

. . .

Sleep Good at Night

It may appear rather unnecessary to highlight but getting adequate rest is important to curb those negative thoughts. Being sleep deprived has become a norm, but it's not a trend that you want to follow. Your 8th-grade health teacher may have been the only person to point this out, but setting regular times that you go to sleep and wake up can work wonders for your mood (we're talking miracles, people, so buy a new plush pillow and sheets that feel like butter to jack up your motivation).

Get Your Hopes Up

Perhaps, you know someone who, when disaster strikes, says the common phrase: "'Guess I shouldn't have gotten my hopes up!" This is possibly one of the most destructive mentalities to have. If you never get your hopes up, what do you have to look forward to? (Walking to the hot dog stand down the street doesn't cut it.) Yes, it's true that sometimes plans fall through but more often than not, they don't. Everyone needs to have meaningful experiences to look forward to. Everyone needs to believe that they, too, can win the game of life (not the board game; although, board games are super fun on rainy days).

CONCLUDING IDEAS

The power of positive thoughts will not be lost on you now that you've discovered the insights of this chapter. While positive thinking cannot solve all your problems, it can lighten the mental and emotional load that you carry every day. Changing a thought can shift the way that you feel and has the power to turn your entire day around. If you did this every day, imagine how different your life would be a year from now. Yes, you would still have trials to deal with, but I'm sure you would deal with them differently.

By employing the techniques that you learned, you can take this power into your own hands. Seemingly impossible things can and will be achieved with positive thinking. There's no reason why you can't be the person who accomplishes the highest of goals. Negative thoughts no longer have to rule your life; you can find new ways to see your circumstances. Sometimes, you're just a tiny thought away from an entirely new uncharted path.

6

GRATITUDE: THE MOST POWERFUL POSITIVE THOUGHT

"Be grateful for what you have; you'll end up having more. If you concentrate on what you don't have, you will never, ever have enough."

— *OPRAH WINFREY*

The long-term benefits of gratitude cannot be underestimated. By investing your energy into developing a consistent perspective that is seeped (like a great cup of tea) in feelings of being grateful, you will see a dramatic turnaround in your quality of life. This practice goes far beyond accepting the common phrase: "Be grateful for what you have." It's a daily cultivation and persistent desire to flood the body with this powerful tonic. If you want to reduce your stress and anxiety, gratitude is one of the most efficient ways to accomplish that goal.

THE ADVANTAGE OF A GRATEFUL LIFE

Have you ever wondered what the secret is to embracing a positive attitude, especially in the middle of trying circumstances? You're definitely not alone. It's seen as quite unusual to respond with peace and grace to a great challenge.

Onlookers will wonder: "How the heck is that guy smiling when he just lost his car in an accident?"

The response will likely be: "I'm alive. That's all that matters. I can always get a new car."

Ah, the wonders of gratitude!

This big picture perspective is what most people long for. Meanwhile, they are often ranting about the credit card bills and the long line at the sandwich shop. Maybe having a better understanding of how gratitude can shift your attitude will be the missing puzzle piece that will have you shouting "hazzah!" (you probably don't ever say that, but you know what I mean).

Sturdy and Restorative Friendships

When you are filled with gratitude, you will want to spread your good mood around like Santa Claus. You'll pick up the phone just to find out how your best friend is doing. You may even strike up the desire to hammer together a tree house that in no way resembles the picture online but makes you feel good about giving back to the Boy Scouts of America (all those little scouts will be amazed that their new tree house somehow isn't falling apart). Yet, that's the power of gratitude: It allows you to make connections and build (not just a tree house) but deep bonds with people. Plus, it feels good knowing that you have made a difference and others look to you as someone they can count on. Everyone could use more of that satisfaction in their lives.

Being Bold and Courageous

Nothing looks better on you than a glowing face filled with confidence. Every one of us has reasons to feel insecure because perfection doesn't exist (yet we all try to acquire it under the false assumption that maybe it is within reach). Confident people don't need perfection; they just need to feel good within their own skin. They are grateful for exactly who they are. The more positivity and confidence you invite into your life, the less likely you are to walk into a room with a sheepish nod wondering who is going to want to talk to you. If you play your cards right and feel gratitude for who you are, the answer is: Every single person in the room.

Frame of Reference

Your point of view is the switch that you can use to eliminate those moments where you feel like Eeyore from *Winnie The Pooh* where there is a dark cloud hanging above your head. No matter how well things go, Eeyore sinks deeper into a pit of despair and doesn't know how to find his way out. Without the right perspective, nothing in your life will really go the way you want it to. Unexpected things happen to everyone, but it's one's mindset that makes all the difference. If only Eeyore would understand all he has to be grateful for, maybe that dark cloud would leave him be.

Erasing Discolored Feelings

It's quite difficult for toxicity to exist in your life if you have a consistent gratitude practice. Any negative emotion can be considered toxic if it is heavily influential on one's actions, thoughts, and words. Keeping these emotions at bay can be a natural outcome of daily engagement with gratitude. It really can start to feel as though the negative emotions feel a great distance away. They will drift off just like "Wilson!" in that movie *Cast Away*.

Upgrade Your Sleeping Rhythms

Gratitude has a huge impact on the quality of the sleep that you get every night. This is because gratitude prompts the hypothalamus to initiate improved control over steady sleeping patterns (Awosika, para. 40). That means feeling grateful means feeling well-rested.

WEAVING GRATITUDE INTO EVERYDAY LIVING

Now that you understand that gratitude is just as powerful as Captain America (and maybe even more!), here's how to incorporate it into your life.

Gratitude Walk

This practice simply entails taking in your surroundings as you walk alone or with someone you love. The more you observe, the more you are grounded in the present moment. Reflect on how this walk makes you feel and why you are deeply grateful for this experience. You can choose to do this practice silently as you simply witness what is happening or you can discuss out loud what you are grateful for.

Thoughts on Gratitude

This exercise is rather simple but effective and encourages you to speak your gratitude out loud. Take a moment to find a spot where you are comfortable and free of interruptions. Picture in your mind's eye the people who fill you with gratitude and then say aloud, "Thank you for this gift of gratitude."

Consider how you have grown over the course of your life and then say aloud, "Thank you for this gift of gratitude."

Acknowledge the fact that there are so many people who had to come together in order for you to exist in this moment and then say aloud, "Thank you for this gift of gratitude."

Think about all the days that lie ahead for you, all the moments and milestones you have yet to experience. Take a deep breath and allow the excitement to well up within you. Breathe out and then say aloud, "Thank you for this gift of gratitude."

Writing With Gratitude

For this activity you can choose from any statement that resonates with you. You simply have to finish the incomplete sentence. This exercise helps to train your brain to look for things that you are grateful for throughout your days.

You can pick from the statements below or you can come up with your own:

- One thing that fills me with gratitude is:
- A recent life experience that has taught me to be grateful is:
- I am grateful for my job because:
- I had a negative experience recently but I am grateful for it because:
- The person in my life that I'm most grateful for is:

- Something in my home that fills me with gratitude is:
- Someone in my life offered me a gift, and I am grateful for it because:
- A friend of mine that I can depend on makes me feel incredibly grateful because:
- Something funny happened this past week that I'm grateful for, and it was:
- Something that surprised me this past week and reminded me how grateful I am was:

Jug of Gratitude

For this exercise, you can purchase a jug that you find appealing or buy a plain one to decorate yourself (if you want to get crafty). You can use whatever materials you like or simply leave the jar as is. Next, tear off three scraps of paper and record on each something that you are grateful for.

You can write down things like: "I am grateful for my beautiful porch where I can sit and read" or "I'm so grateful that I have a supportive community when I need a boost."

Each day, add three more things you are grateful for. This simple practice will serve as a reminder that no matter how complicated life gets, there's always reasons to be grateful. When you are feeling upset or discouraged by life, pull out one of the scraps of paper to rekindle the gratitude that you have already cultivated.

Reflective Pastimes Journaling

Often when you reflect on your past, all you see are the things that you regret and all those moments when you should have said or done something differently. This exercise is meant to train your brain to see your past differently. If you aren't so bogged down by regret, you have more internal space for gratitude.

To get started, pull out a notebook and a pen. Write about one of your happiest memories, including as many details as you would like. The point of this exercise is to feel gratitude welling up within you. It does not matter so much if there are some things missing from the actual events. Do this writing exercise for about ten minutes.

The second part of this exercise will ask you to write about something that you normally reflect on with disdain. Write about it and try your best to search for a reason to be grateful. Is there something that you've overlooked? Did that situation help you learn a lesson? Was it a necessary step in your life's journey? Do this half of the writing exercise for around ten minutes as well.

The purpose here is to experience gratitude and do the work of looking for it as well. Then, you can begin to find gratitude in all areas of your life, no matter if they come out of a good or bad situation.

FINAL THOUGHTS

Gratitude is a fairly simple practice that has profound results. Give yourself time to focus on what you have rather than what is missing from your life. You will see that life can be filled with joy when gratitude is at the forefront of your mind. You learned practices in this chapter that can help you cultivate gratitude daily. The techniques provided can have a huge impact on the way that you feel as you go about your day.

Gratitude is like a boat that carries you from one side of the shore to the other. It can take you on a journey far beyond the confines that you are accustomed to. Gratitude can expand your awareness of all the possibilities that life has to offer.

After all, it's quite difficult to sulk when you are meditating on thoughts of gratitude. You may not have exercised this muscle of gratitude much in the past but now is your chance to be transformed by this force of good. Take advantage of the exercises in this chapter and see what these new habits can bring you. Gratitude will take you as far beyond the horizon as you let it.

7

EAT, MEDITATE, AND EXERCISE STRESS AWAY

"Set your mind on a definite goal and observe how quickly the world stands aside to let you pass."

— *NAPOLEON HILL, THINK AND GROW RICH*

I t's amazing what a nourishing diet can do for your depression, anxiety, and stress levels. When you make conscious choices about the foods you eat, you will feel a difference in your body and mind. According to Pomfrey (n.d.), "A study published by the *American Journal of Psychiatry* examined the dietary habits and levels of depression and anxiety of over 1,000 women over 10 years. The women who ate a 'western' diet of fast food, processed foods, refined grains, sweets and beer were more likely to be depressed or anxious than those who ate a more 'traditional' diet—vegetables, fruit, whole grains, meat and fish" (Pomfrey, para. 5).

In addition to a good diet, meditation can also help you reduce your stress and anxiety levels. We've discussed meditation briefly in previous chapters, but here we will really dive into the practice, and I'll share some solid techniques for how you can develop your own meditation routine. Although you may think that you have to become some mystical guru to achieve the benefits of meditation, well, don't get carried away on me. Everyone from pro athletes to Oprah meditate, so you can, too!

Next, exercise is an almost surefire way to reduce your stress levels. Exercise increases the production of endorphins, which will make you feel like a real-life version of Road Runner from *Looney Toons* (the point here being that you'll never want to stop running). There's that all too common phrase that comes up when discussing stress: flight-or-fight response. This creates a constant state of stress that doesn't let up until you tell your body that you're in the clear. Regular exercise can flip that switch generating a serene response that makes you feel like you're on a beach in Puerto Rico (as opposed to being on a set of train tracks bracing for impact). See the difference?

Exercise can help you to tune out everything and focus your attention only on your exerted effort. This focused attention can remain with you throughout the day and help you to maintain a sense of peace as you manage your daily tasks.

You can use these three habits to create a sort of Power Rangers "It's Morphin Time!" scenario where all three come together to create a better you.

SUSTENANCE TO SOOTHE THE ANXIOUS AND STRESSFUL BODY

It's easy to get into the mindset that you don't have the time or money to eat healthy, but what you really can't afford is to damage your future health. You can be certain that attempting to reverse poor health decisions will cost you far more than choosing the right foods right now. You don't have to completely overhaul your diet all at once like *Extreme Makeover: Home Edition*, either. You can make small choices daily that add up, over time, to a better diet.

To soothe your stress and anxiety, try incorporating these optimal nourishments into your diet:

- dark chocolate
- bananas
- milk
- leafy greens
- oranges, grapefruit, and strawberries

- avocados
- water
- fish
- whole grains
- warm foods like soup, steel-cut oats, or tea (Kennedy, 2019)

On the other hand, here are the things that you should avoid just like you dodge Aunt Karen at Thanksgiving:

- alcohol
- processed sugar
- caffeine (Kennedy, 2019)

USING MEDITATION TO HUSH YOUR TENSION

By meditating frequently, you will start to notice subtle changes in the way that you cope with problems. You will naturally feel a greater sense of ease as you move through your day. There will be a balance within like you've never known. You will be like Mr. Miyagi from the *Karate Kid*, full of zen and inner power. As peace replenishes your frazzled nerves, remember that you had it within you all along to feel this way.

Here are the benefits of meditation:

- living in the present moment
- stronger awareness on how to mitigate stress
- activating a new take on a difficult circumstance
- developing skills for improved stress reduction
- seeing a positive change in your creative pursuits
- letting go of negative thoughts and emotions
- feeling more patient and building tolerance (Mayo Clinic Staff, 2020)

Now, all you need to do is, you know, actually meditate.

There are many ways to step into your meditation practice, and you may find that more than one way works well for you. Give each of the below exercises a try and see which ones fit best into your lifestyle. Keep in mind that these are meant to be simple techniques that aren't meant to complicate your day. You can engage in these practices whenever you have a few spare moments or you can schedule them into your day. All that matters is that you commit to being present with yourself.

Intentional Breathing

We've discussed the power of intentional breathing previously, and in this practice, you will focus solely on your breath. Even just a few minutes of this practice can reset your mind and aid you in being more productive. All you have to do is give your attention to your breathing. Be sure to inhale and exhale out of your nose. Notice the oxygen going in and out of your body. As you slow down the pace of your breath, feel a strong energy cleansing all your organs. When your thoughts drift away, ever so gently bring them back to the movement of your breath. On your final exhale, simply open your eyes and go about the rest of your day (Mayo Clinic Staff, 2020).

Inner Devotion Meditation

With this meditation, your attention will be on feelings of love and gratitude. Close your eyes and imagine a glowing light of love at the center of your chest. Picture this light growing and spreading across your body. Feel the energy of love filling you up with each breath that you take. Imagine that your breath is the energy that helps this light to grow until your entire body is consumed in this beautiful energy. Simply sit and let yourself be consumed by this love. When you feel ready, repeat this same process but imagine that the glowing light at the center of your chest is gratitude (Mayo Clinic Staff, 2020).

Head-to-Toe Sweep

This exercise will help you to be more present with your body. You will build more awareness of both pleasant and unpleasant feelings. All you have to do is sit comfortably and close your eyes. Take a deep breath in and out, relaxing all the muscles in your body. Start with the top of your head and slowly move your awareness down your body. Go at your own pace and be aware of the feelings that arise.

As you do this, remain conscious of what feels good and what feels uncomfortable. Continue to move your awareness down your body and stop in the areas where you feel discomfort. Picture the powerful force of your inhale gathering this dense energy. Now imagine your exhale removing this discomfort from your body. See the energy leaving your body like smoke wafting away from a campfire. After a few breaths, notice if the discomfort lightens or changes at all. Continue down your body until you reach your toes. Take three deep breaths and slowly open your eyes (Mayo Clinic Staff, 2020).

Magnetic Mantra

Spoken words have an incredible effect on your mindset and emotions (remember our discussion about self-talk? Same idea here). By utilizing mantras, you can achieve dramatic results in every area of your life. According to Boyle (2017), "Mantras not only stimulate the right and left sides of your brain, but repetitive usage of mantras can alter brain waves from a beta state (when you are super focused) to a more theta state (relaxed). Theta states raise your level of awareness and consciousness, providing a sense of calm and ease" (Boyle, p.19, para. 2).

To evoke this sense of calm, try this mantra meditation practice:

1. First, say aloud the mantra that you will be using for this practice: *Sa Ta Na Ma* (pronounced, saa taa naa

maa). Repeat this a few times until you get the hang of it.

2. This mantra represents the circle of life: being born, facing death, and returning to earth through reincarnation. It's a cyclical metamorphosis and has a strong emphasis on the power of change. This cycle also represents the phases that we go through in life and how change is an ever-present feature.

3. This mantra can be used to initiate the death cycle where you are aiming to let go of something negative, such as anxiety. This mantra can act as a reset button to help you eradicate all thought patterns and imbalances that are holding you back.

4. All you need to do for this practice is repeat the mantra aloud. Ideally, you would practice this for about five minutes. While you say the mantra aloud, close your eyes and picture one thing that you would like to expel from your life. If this is too much, feel free to simply focus your attention on repeating the mantra.

5. Once you are finished, take a deep breath and open your eyes. (Boyle, p.210, para. 3)

CULTIVATING HEALTH WITH ACTIVE MOVEMENT

Regular exercise can improve the overall quality of your life by helping you sweat out your stress and anxiety. You may even see that your responses to stressful circumstances are different, too. You will feel more grounded and better able to take what is thrown your way, because, darn it, you just did an hour of cardio and nothing can stop you now! Never underestimate the power of a pair of jogging shorts and a few laps around the block. You might just have a dreams-really-do-come-true moment.

Yet, the trouble with regular exercise is following through with it. To help get you going, there's a concept called SMART goals, and the reason this is so handy is because they give you a way to track your progress (Mayo Clinic, 2020). SMART stands for: specific, measurable, attainable, relevant, and time-limited goals (Mayo Clinic, 2020). An example of this would be: I will wake up an hour early three times a week to attend Zumba class. By doing so, my goal is to increase my productivity by thirty percent and to achieve this percentage in the next ninety days.

Instead of writing out vague goals that offer fleeting hopes that things might change someday (New Year's resolutions, anyone?), SMART goals give you a more concrete approach to achieving your specific fitness goals.

Also, keep an eye out for a friend who likes the same exercise routines as you. Sometimes, part of the goal-setting process is having someone alongside you with the same outcome in mind. Because you both have skin in the game, you're more likely to follow through. If you can't find a current friend who would be interested, check out some local meetups, and you may just discover a new work-out buddy (Mayo Clinic, 2020).

Sometimes, it can be hard to stick with your exercise routine if it doesn't offer much excitement or variety. For example, if you have a treadmill shoved in the corner of a room overloaded with paperwork, you may associate exercise with this unsightly arrangement. Look up some new exercise equipment and machines, and you might discover your love of Pilates or even boxing (Mayo Clinic, 2020).

The time you need to devote to regular exercise depends on the type of exercise you are doing. For example, if you choose to stick with an aerobic workout, it's good to aim for two and a half hours of exercise per week (Jackson, May/June 2013). If you opt for yoga instead, you can choose a range between two to four hours of exercise per week (Jackson, May/June 2013).

When you're just starting out, go easy on yourself, as you can create more stress by trying to stick to time frames or can wear yourself out. If you find that even the idea of exercise is stressful, give yourself permission to start slow. Maybe just begin with one hour per week and gradually work up from there. Even the greatest of athletes had to start by practicing one free throw shot.

YOGA FOR REDUCING YOUR STRESS LEVELS

Yoga has the power to be more than just a workout. It can be a powerful tool for successfully managing life's many difficulties. The term yoga means to "yoke" or to unify the mind, body, and soul (Scott, 2020). The reason this is so important is because your experiences and feelings can be so taxing that you end up feeling like three separate parts. And when you are not unified, you cannot operate as a whole person. Yoga helps you connect your mind, body, and soul so that you can find a strength within that you never knew you had.

By bringing these severed parts of the self back together again, you are able to move forward from a grounded place that is full of peace. This is how yoga can be used to diminish stress and anxiety levels and return you to a natural state of well-being.

Yoga is a combination of mindfulness practices, physical effort, deep breathing, spirituality, and self-love (Scott, 2020). These are just some of the perks of yoga:

- decreased blood pressure
- improved sleeping patterns
- a decline of cortisol in the body

- lower levels of stress and anxiety
- reduced muscle strain and tightness
- greater strength and elasticity
- delayed signs of growing older
- alleviated symptoms of both allergies and asthma (Scott, 2020)

With a list of benefits such as this (and believe me, I'm *not* over-selling them), it is quite obvious why yoga is more than just a form of exercise. It is a way of life where its practice seeps into all areas of your life. Not only will you feel more connected to yourself, but you will feel greater ease around others as well. Yoga increases your desire to live with patience, empathy, and love, which are all important when maintaining a calm, peaceful self.

Understand it may take some time for your body to adjust to the practice because it is hard work. It's best not to go it alone, and you can either find a local yoga class or studio or find online yoga teachers.

CLOSING THOUGHTS

It's quite surprising to learn all the ways that you can change your outlook by switching up a few habits. Your diet, exercise routine, and meditation practice all have the capacity to change the way you feel about yourself. When you feel differently about yourself, the sky is truly the limit (unless you're a seasoned astronaut, then maybe the galaxy is the limit). Nothing is too far out of reach as long as you are willing to put in the time and effort.

Much of the work that you have done throughout this book has helped to lessen or manage stressors. Your natural tendencies probably create a lot of stress in your life (and you're not alone). Most people really have no idea how to better handle the stress that comes flying at them. You have an advantage over most by holding this book in your hands. Learn to make small changes in your life, and you will see that the smallest steps can lead to big changes.

8

BATTLE STRESS WITH ART AND MUSIC

"If each day is a gift, I'd like to know where I can return Mondays."

— *JOHN WAGNER*

According to a study performed by the researchers at the prestigious Stanford University, "listening to music seems to be able to change brain functioning to the same extent as medication" (University Of Nevada, Reno, para. 2). We all know that medication has the power to change the influence of stress hormones on the body. If music has the power to do the same, then it's entirely possible to turn to this resource without the side effects that are caused by medication.

The sound of music (not talking about the movie, here, but hey, it does have a great soundtrack) can shift your emotions, which reduces the harmful effects that your stress hormones have on your body. Your thoughts gradually slow down and your breathing lightens as your muscles loosen up. You have no doubt already experienced the positive benefits of music on your stress hormones. Think about the times when your favorite sad song hits you right in that tender place in your heart. Do you ever find yourself tearing up? This experience is a natural release of stress, and the benefits can be felt immediately.

Classical music, especially, or other types of instrumental melodies can slow down the surge of stress moving through the body. The frequencies of the music have a gentle and peaceful influence over the body's impulse to give in to stress. According to Collingwood (2020), research also shows that "music's form and structure can bring order and security to disabled and distressed children. It encourages coordination and communication, so improves their quality of life" (Collingwood, para.9). If you think about it, this is the reason why so many parents and teachers fight to keep music classes in schools.

Plus, the healing power of music isn't just for kids; it's for adults, too. Music isn't just pure entertainment. It is a form of restoration that can support you throughout your life.

Music isn't the only way that you can manage your stress as visual art has been shown to do the same. According to Chopra and Sehgal (2017), "Just like physical exercise, creative stimulation engages and focuses our minds on the task at hand—and distracts us from feelings of stress and anxiety." It doesn't matter if you are scrapbooking or creating a pot from clay, if you are melting into your creative state of bliss, you are reducing the power that stress has on your life. So, whether you choose to take up knitting, sewing, painting, or sculpting, you can find ways to turn your anxiety and stress into a positive work of art.

Investing your time into creativity can also prove to be useful in that you are better able to connect and understand others. Sharing the same musical taste, playing the same instrument, or even painting in a group can help you forge important connections. Just think about your favorite art class back in elementary school, and how nice it was to sit with friends and create cool things.

Remember, everyone has the right to create even if it's nothing more than a homemade candle. If it means something to you, don't shy away from it just because you haven't done it before and aren't an expert. Refrain from dismissing the arts because you assume that you aren't creative.

Everyone is creative (yes, even you). It's just that most of us have shut down our creative centers. It doesn't matter to what degree you are creative, all that counts is that you are using art as a way to find happiness.

IDEAS FOR USING MUSIC TO FACE STRESS EFFECTIVELY

Don't hesitate to release your stress by cranking up one of your favorite songs or simply using one of the ideas listed below on how to incorporate music into your stress-reduction plan.

Learn an Instrument

One way to get some sweet tunes in your life is by taking up an instrument. Look for tutorials online and see if you can teach yourself to play a song using a flute, a guitar, a piano, or drums. If you take the time to do so, you will notice a decrease in your stress levels.

Fill the Mundane With Music

Look for a playlist online and listen to it while you do a mundane task. You might even enjoy a seemingly boring task a little bit more. Facing boredom can be stressful, especially if you have to work on a tedious project. If you get distracted by music with lyrics, look for instrumental playlists. You might find that it's easier to focus and the time will pass more quickly, which can also lessen the tension you feel.

Community Music

If you enjoy group settings, consider joining a drum circle, a singing group, or a music class. You can also look into local music workshops. There really is something out there for everyone, no matter skill level, talent, or taste.

If you have a knack for playing an instrument, you might consider teaching a class as part of the summer program through your local park or school district. This can be another great way to reduce your stress levels because giving back to your community is incredibly rewarding. There are options to teach adults, teens, or young children depending on your preference.

Attend Live Music Shows

Look up local theatre events and see if there is a concert or musical coming up. The effort that goes into these performances is something to appreciate. Being a witness to this collective use of musical creativity is worth the money you spend for a ticket. It will also give you something to look forward to, which can help carry you through stressful moments.

Up Your Amateur Musician Status

Maybe performing for a live audience has always interested you but you don't necessarily have the desire to be a full-time musician. There are plenty of local coffee shops, bars, or fine dining restaurants that will seek out musicians to play for their customers. Landing a music gig is similar to applying for a regular job. If you have the experience, references, professionalism, and talent they are looking for, you could be the lucky one to make this dream a reality.

ART THERAPY SOLUTIONS FOR SUBDUING STRESS AND ANXIETY

Art therapy is a tool that you can use to find the emotional release that you are looking for. Sometimes, writing or speaking about your stress and anxiety falls short, and you aren't able to fully process what you're feeling. Art therapy, however, can act as a bridge that helps you to cross over into the unexplored regions of yourself.

All art is simply the human condition being expressed through various forms. The products of your art therapy don't ever have to be shown to anyone nor do they have to be praiseworthy. The aim is for you to learn more about yourself and to find ways to release emotions that are trapped within you.

You will discover that you are far more complex than you realized and more creative than you expected. The self-exploration through art therapy is truly endless. Be open to the process, and you'll find that it's worth the time you put in.

Although art therapy is often used to help children or those who have suffered from trauma, there is no reason why you, too, can't use this healing tool. Art therapy can help you:

- discover feelings that have been hidden away in your mind

- create strong feelings of achievement as you work on completing a project
- build a safe space to process and release difficult emotions
- reduce stress and find peace in your spirit (Cohen, 2018)

Below are some simple art exercises to get you thinking about the cool things you can create and do to alleviate stress.

Blind Art

This first exercise is quite simple. When you're feeling anxious, grab a sheet of paper, colored pencils, and some tape. Secure your paper to a table with the tape.

Take a moment to reflect on the anxiety you are feeling. What color do you think best expresses this feeling? Take your chosen colored pencil, close your eyes, and let it glide across the page. All you are doing is making one long continuous swirling motion on the page. Allow your anxiety to float onto the page. Trust that your anxiety is leaving your body through the action of taking the pencil to paper. When you feel ready, stop drawing and take a look at what you've created.

You can now grab other pencils and continue expressing your anxiety on the paper. When you finish, simply reflect on what this experience was like for you. Do you feel any differently? Did anything come up for you that you'd like to explore? Was a particular memory or insecurity rising to the surface? Spend five to ten minutes writing these thoughts down or considering them. When you finish, take a deep breath and appreciate yourself for taking the time to let go of these emotions (Tartakovsky, 2018).

A Themed Collage

Bring together some magazines, a scrapbook or a poster board, some glue, and writing utensils. Choose a theme that you want to work with. Maybe you want to explore social settings that trigger your anxiety or how stressed out you feel at work. Whatever theme you decide on, creating a collage based on it can help you to wade through some of the stressful feelings about it. Go about cutting out images, words, or scenes from your magazines and artfully glue them to your scrapbook or board.

Having the space to work through these complex emotions in a creative way can be just the release that you have been looking for. You don't have to go to a retreat center perched on a serene mountaintop to get the clarity you are looking for. With openness and a little glue, you can find it right at your dining room table. It's okay if you feel silly at first but don't let that slow down your progress.

Once you finish, look over your work and try to understand what is being expressed on the page. You may find yourself making connections or understanding yourself in a way that you hadn't before. Ponder how you are feeling after doing this activity and feel free to journal about this if you need to. Art therapy will take you on an emotional journey. It can be quite startling to realize how overcome you are by sadness or joy. It's important to work through these feelings to gain the full effect that art therapy has to offer (Tartakovsky, 2018).

How Anxiety Colors Perception

For this next exercise, you can choose whatever art supplies you would like, such as paint, crayons, colored pencils, or even clay. Next, ask yourself how anxiety shapes your world. Get curious about how anxiety influences your choices and how you hold yourself. This isn't about judgment; it's simply about being honest. Finding the truth about your anxiety and how it shapes your life can aid you in overcoming it. The more obscure anxiety is the more likely it will have control over your life.

There are no rules for this exercise. You can draw realistic figures, make collages, or create an object out of clay. If you don't know where to begin, simply start with a feeling. Try to express that feeling through your artistic medium of choice and then move onto the next feeling. There is no right way of going about this project. The end result can be a very abstract piece that is filled with hidden meanings or a literal drawing or painting of a specific place that triggers your anxiety. When you finish, the hope is that you have a better understanding of how anxiety influences you.

You are not your anxiety, but it is a big part of your life. It's important to have a thorough understanding of your anxiety and how it can often stop you from living the life that you deserve (Tartakovsky, 2018). This exercise allows you to explore how your anxiety shows up in your life so that you can understand and deal with it better.

Find Your Radiance With Adult Coloring

One simple way to bring art into your life is to go out and get some adult coloring books. Simple coloring can be a little easier to fit into your day as opposed to a big art project. Even just 15 minutes of coloring a day can make all the difference in how you feel. You may be surprised by how much you enjoy the experience of coloring between the lines.

Even though it may not seem like much, you are still creating something. The way that you fill in the colors on the page is a form of self-expression. You may feel a little strange when you sit down to color as this is often seen as a children's activity. However, adult coloring books are becoming increasingly popular. Resist the urge to be self-conscious and think about the benefits that can come from these small pockets of time that you spend with yourself. It's not about how this activity is viewed by others; it's about finding the healing modality that works for you (Marder, 2019).

Draw or Doodle

Time spent doodling or drawing is a wonderful way to express yourself. Whether you decide to draw funny characters or doodle pictures of trees, you are taking the time to express your thoughts and feelings and focus on yourself. There's something very gratifying about putting pen to paper and creating something unique. It doesn't have to be anything special, just experiment. (Marder, 2019).

If you are trying to draw specific objects or characters, maybe look up tutorials online. You can also find tutorial books that walk you through the process of bringing a character to life. If guided drawing seems above your art skill-set, then doodling is a great alternative. You can't go wrong with either as they both can support you in your search for relief from stress and anxiety (Marder, 2019).

Tracing Your Stress

For this exercise, grab a sketchbook or a sheet of paper and simply draw what you are feeling. In whatever form it emerges, allow it to come. Maybe there are things that you can't say to your boss, so express them on the page instead. Are there things that happened today or this week that you've been ruminating on? Draw those, too, in whatever form they come (Scott, 2020).

When you feel stressed about work or your home life and nothing seems to be going right, it can be helpful to have an outlet for these intense emotions. You may be feeling agitated, overwhelmed, angry, or impatient. It's important to acknowledge any of these negative feelings and give yourself the permission to feel it all. When you give yourself the space to feel these unpleasant emotions, you are slowly letting them go. You will no doubt feel better by the end of your time working on this project. Even if you look down at your page and see nothing but lines and scribbles, you still found a way to express your emotions. That's exactly what art therapy is for (Scott, 2020).

FURTHER OBSERVATIONS

Before reading this chapter, you may not have given music or art much thought in connection with helping you manage your stress. Every technique and art exercise we discussed may not work for you. What's important, though, is that you give it the old college try. You never know if you will actually dig collaging or coloring unless you actually try. (Remember what your mom often said about unfamiliar foods: "How can you know you don't like it if you've never tasted it?")

Don't forget that the way that you feel after doing the exercises is the most important thing. Also, don't allow fear or shame stop you from diving into art or music projects. It doesn't matter if you draw like a kindergarten or like Van Gough or if you sing like a tone-deaf dog or like Mariah Carey. If music or art helps you achieve an emotional release and feel better, then it's worth it. You've done your part to better manage your stress and anxiety.

Creativity has a long track record of being a life-changing vehicle for healing and defeating stress and anxiety. So, why not accept that creativity has the potential to lift so much of what you are carrying? You might see that in your creative expression, you find a strength that you never knew existed.

CONCLUSION

Throughout the pages of this book, you uncovered various aspects of life that can negatively and positively influence your stress and anxiety levels. We touched on how stress and anxiety affect the body. You learned how to effectively declutter your life at work and at home. You discovered how easily the body can be influenced by your environment in both helpful and harmful ways.

You realized that confidence is your superpower in social situations and that social anxiety doesn't have to take over your life. You now understand how bad influences and toxic individuals have no place on your priority list. Even though some toxic people may always be in your life because they are family, you know how to set boundaries and stick to them. You may work with some toxic people as well, but your standards remain the same. You know how to manage these people without it affecting the quality of your life or work.

Positive thinking and reflections on gratitude were key points that were highlighted. You read about how negative thinking can be one of the most harmful habits you engage in. You've been exposed to various techniques that can help you mitigate your stress and overcome the anxiety that has debilitated you in the past. No stressor is beyond your ability to cope and manage. You can learn to apply all the techniques offered in this book to better handle the stress that comes your way.

You uncovered the power of food, exercise, and meditation, and why they are all needed to live a better and more positive lifestyle. You now see how a poor diet and a lack of an exercise routine can stand in the way of you attaining happiness. You see how meditation can have a positive, lasting impact. Now, you see that carving out time for these activities is not only possible but it is necessary.

Lastly, you connected with the power of music and art to lessen your stress and anxiety levels to find peace within. Art and music are not just for kids nor are they purely for the elite among us. They both can have a place in your world as you learn to overcome and conquer your stress and anxiety. You have the knowledge and understanding that you can utilize these creative resources to make a better life for yourself.

Continue to use the exercises throughout the book to enhance your life. Anxiety and stress no longer have to be a way of life for you. You have the power to change how you respond to the circumstances of your everyday life. The exercises in this book can help to lighten the load so that you don't have to struggle through your days. Know that freedom is within reach. Know and that you really can have the life that you've always dreamed of. Anxiety and stress don't have to keep you from truly living anymore.

Believe that you have what it takes. Believe that you are more than your thoughts, feelings, and overwhelming circumstances. You already have all that you need to be great in this world. Remember to resist defining yourself by who you've always been. Instead, define yourself by who you know you are deep down, by all that has yet to emerge from within you. Go live your best life and when you need it, this book is always here for you (just like Mom is).

Thank you for taking the time to read this book. If you found it enjoyable, please take a moment to leave a favorable review on Amazon. I appreciate your feedback, too, as this helps other readers to get the help they need to overcome their stress and anxiety. Sharing is caring, as they say.

Thank you for reading my book. If you have enjoyed reading it perhaps you would like to leave a star rating and a review for me on Amazon? It really helps support writers like myself create more books. You can leave a review for me by scanning the QR code below;

Thank you so much.

Martin Moriarty

REFERENCES

Alton, L. (2017, June 22). Why clutter is killing your focus (and how to fix it): How to lose the stuff that's messing with your mental clarity and hurting your health. Better. https://www.nbcnews.com/better/health/why-clutter-killing-your-focus-how-fix-it-ncna775531

Alvord, M., & Halfond, R. (2019, October 28). What's the difference between stress and anxiety? Knowing the difference can ensure you get the help you need. American Psychological Association. https://www.apa.org/topics/stress-anxiety-difference#:~:text=People%20under%20stress%20experience%20mental,the%20absence%20of%20a%20stressor.

American Brain Society. (2019, May 1). Stress, the silent killer. https://americanbrainsociety.org/stress-the-silent-killer/

Anxiety and Depression Association of America. (n.d.). Facts and statistics. ADAA. https://adaa.org/about-adaa/press-room/facts-statistics

Anxiety Canada. (n.d.). Tool 1: Real life exposures (building your confidence). http://www.anxietycanada.com/articles/tool-1-real-life-exposures-building-your-confidence/?_ga=2.199131119.1914239337.1591619335-446207806.1591619335

Anxiety Canada. (n.d.). Tool 2: Mental exposures (building your confidence). http://www.anxietycanada.com/articles/tool-2-mental-exposures-building-your-confidence/?_ga=2.199131119.1914239337.1591619335-446207806.1591619335

Anxiety Canada. (n.d.). Tool 4: Resisting the quickfix. http://www.anxietycanada.com/articles/tool-4-resisting-the-quick-fix/?_ga=2.199131119.1914239337.1591619335-446207806.1591619335

Anxiety Canada. (n.d.). Tool 5: Managing worries (Building your confidence). http://www.anxietycanada.com/articles/tool-5-managing-worries-building-your-confidence/?_ga=2.199131119.1914239337.1591619335-446207806.1591619335

Awosika, L. O. (2019, September 22). Transforming your health and well-being through positive thinking and stress relieve. Thrive Global. https://thriveglobal.com/stories/transforming-your-health-and-well-being-through-positive-thinking-and-stress-relieve/

Blake, J. (n.d.). How to deal with the toxic people you can't cut out of your life. Bolde. https://www.bolde.com/deal-toxic-people-cant-cut-life/

Boyle, S. (2017). Mantras made easy: Mantras for happiness peace prosperity and more. Adams Media.

Boynton, E. (2020, April 29). Feeling stressed or lonely? Here's how practicing art and music can help. Right as Rain by UW Medicine. https://rightasrain.uwmedicine.org/mind/mental-health/art-and-music

Brenner, A. (2018, February 22). 7 Strategies to deal with difficult family members: Here's how to maintain your integrity in family relationships. Psychology Today. https://www.psychologytoday.com/us/blog/in-flux/201802/7-strategies-deal-difficult-family-members

Cassibry, K. (2016, September 20). Understanding the vicious cycle of stress and low self-esteem. Inpathy Bulletin. https://inpathybulletin.com/understanding-cycle-stress-low-self-esteem/

Chokshi, N. (2019, April 25). Americans are among the most stressed people in the world poll finds. The New York Times. https://www.nytimes.com/2019/04/25/us/americans-stressful.html

Chopra, D., & Sehgal, K. (2017, September 15). Science shows how creativity can reduce stress: When you're stressed out try writing a song. It can improve your health. Entrepreneur. https://www.entrepreneur.com/article/300347

Chowdhury, M.R. (2020, December 5). The neuroscience of gratitude and how it affects anxiety and grief. Positive Psychology. https://positivepsychology.com/neuroscience-of-gratitude/

Clay, K. (n.d.). How to deal with toxic people...in your family. What She Say. https://whatshesay.com/how-to-deal-with-toxic-people-in-your-family/

Clear, J. (n.d.). How to be confident and reduce stress in 2 minutes per day. Lifehack. https://www.lifehack.org/336198/how-confident-and-reduce-stress-2-minutes-per-day

Cohen, M. A. (2018, July 10). Creativity and recovery: The mental health benefits of art therapy. RTOR. https://www.rtor.org/2018/07/10/benefits-of-art-therapy/

Collingwood, J. (2020, July 29). The power of music to reduce stress. Psych Central. https://psychcentral.com/lib/the-power-of-music-to-reduce-stress/

Creel, R. (n.d.). 5 Tips to get organized and reduce stress. Smead. https://www.smead.com/hot-topics/get-organized-1002.asp

Cuncic, A. (2020, March 20). Social anxiety activities to get better. Very Well Mind. https://www.verywellmind.com/social-anxiety-disorder-tips-3024209

Dienstman, A.M. (2018, August 25). How to build a social circle full of positive people: Attracting quality people starts with taking responsibility for your actions and how they affect those around you. Goodnet. https://www.goodnet.org/articles/how-to-build-social-circle-full-positive-people

Doyle, S. (n.d.). 10 Reasons why you should avoid negative people. Lifehack. https://www.lifehack.org/352233/10-reasons-why-you-should-avoid-negative-people

Elkin, A. (n.d.). Express gratitude and reduce stress. Dummies. https://www.dummies.com/health/mental-health/stress-management/express-gratitude-and-reduce-stress/

Emery L.R. (2018, June 12). 7 Ways to shut down the negative voice in your head. Bustle. https://www.bustle.com/p/7-ways-to-get-rid-of-negative-thoughts-according-to-experts-9103649

Fowler, P. (n.d.). How cleaning and organizing can improve your physical and mental health: Organizing your home, office, and even mind can improve your happiness, your relationships, and these other 5 aspects of your life. Shape. https://www.shape.com/lifestyle/mind-and-body/how-cleaning-and-organizing-can-improve-your-physical-and-mental-health

Funny quotes about stress. (2020, June 11). Poem of quotes. https://www.poemofquotes.com/funny-quotes/stress-quotes-2.php

Group, E. (2018, Jul 8). Environmental Stress: How it affects your health. Global Healing. https://globalhealing.com/natural-health/what-is-environmental-stress/

Headspace. (n.d.). Relaxation meditation for stress relief. https://www.headspace.com/meditation/relaxation

Healthline. (2017, June 5). The effects of stress on your body. https://www.healthline.com/health/stress/effects-on-body#1

Healthline Editorial Team. (2017, August 3). Anxiety causes: What causes anxiety disorders? Healthline. https://www.healthline.com/health/anxiety-causes

Hill, Napoleon. (2005). Think and grow rich: The landmark best-seller--now revised and updated for the 21st century. Jeremy P. Tarcher/Penguin.

History.com Editors. (2020, June 29). Amelia Earhart Disappears. History. https://www.history.com/this-day-in-history/amelia-earhart-disappears

Holland, K. (2020, June 23). Everything you need to know about anxiety. Healthline. https://www.healthline.com/health/anxiety

Hurst, K. (n.d.). 8 Toxic people you should just get rid of. The Law Of Attraction. https://www.thelawofattraction.com/8-toxic-people-just-get-rid/

Jackson, E. (2013, May/June). Stress relief: The role of exercise in stress management. ACSM's Health & Fitness Journal. https://journals.lww.com/acsm-healthfitness/fulltext/2013/05000/stress_reliefthe_role_of_exercise_in_stress.6.aspx

Jamal, M. (2019, January 15). 6 Tips to eliminate negative thoughts (backed by research). Thrive Global. https://thriveglobal.com/stories/6-tips-to-eliminate-negative-thoughts-backed-by-research/

Kehoe J. (n.d.). 5 Techniques to eliminate negative thinking. Learn Mind Power. https://www.learnmindpower.com/importance-of-eliminating-negative-thinking/

Kennedy, K. (2019, May 1). The ultimate diet plan for a happier, less-stressed you: How stress affects your diet, the best and worst foods to eat when you're frazzled, and more. Everyday Health. https://www.everydayhealth.com/wellness/united-states-of-stress/ultimate-diet-guide-stress-management/

Lechner, T. (2019, June 24). How to reduce stress through positive thinking: 5 Methods. Chopra. https://chopra.com/articles/how-to-reduce-stress-through-positive-thinking-5-methods

Lieberstein, P. (Writer), & Blitz, J. (Director). (2009, February 1). Stress Relief [Season 5, Episodes 14/15]. Daniels, Greg. (Creator). The Office. Los Angeles, CA:NBC Studios.

Locke, R. (n.d.). 15 Signs of negative people. Lifehack. https://www.lifehack.org/293018/15-signs-negative-people

Marder, L. (2019, March 4). Relieve stress and anxiety by creating art. Live About Dot Com. https://www.liveabout.com/relieve-stress-and-anxiety-with-art-4111397

Martinez, N. (2020, July 29). How to surround yourself with positive people: Learn how to surround yourself with positive people who will help bring out your full potential. Everyday Power. https://everydaypower.com/surround-yourself-with-positive-people/

Mayo Clinic Staff. (2020, April 22). Meditation: A simple fast way to reduce stress. Mayo Clinic. https://www.mayoclinic.org/tests-procedures/meditation/in-depth/meditation/art-20045858

Mayo Clinic Staff. (2020, August 18). Exercise and stress: Get moving to manage stress. Mayo Clinic. https://www.mayoclinic.org/healthy-lifestyle/stress-management/in-depth/exercise-and-stress/art-20044469

Mayo Clinic Staff. (2020, January 21). Positive thinking: Stop negative self-talk to reduce stress. https://www.mayoclinic.org/

healthy-lifestyle/stress-management/in-depth/positive-thinking/art-20043950

McClanahan, J. (2020, June 8). Dealing with toxic people you can't just cut out forever. Scary Mommy. https://www.scarymommy.com/dealing-with-toxic-people/

McCormick, J. (n.d.). How to declutter your life and reduce stress (the ultimate guide). Lifehack. https://www.lifehack.org/articles/lifestyle/how-to-declutter-your-life-and-reduce-stress.html

Medical News Today. (2020, Jan 11). What to know about anxiety. https://www.medicalnewstoday.com/articles/323454

Mental Health Foundation. (n.d.). Mental Health Statistics: Stress. https://www.mentalhealth.org.uk/statistics/mental-health-statistics-stress

Mental Health Foundation. (n.d.). Stress. https://www.mentalhealth.org.uk/a-to-z/s/stress

Nick, A. (2019, October 22). Why should you get rid of negative people from your life? Negative people are like thorns that you need to remove from your life. Here are some reasons why. Thrive Global. https://thriveglobal.com/stories/why-should-you-get-rid-of-negative-people-from-your-life/

Oakley, A. (2016, August 29). How to deal with negative family members. Inner Peace Now. https://www.innerpeacenow.com/inner-peace-blog/how-to-deal-with-negative-family-members

Oppland, M. (2020, April 23). 13 Most popular gratitude exercises & activities. Positive Psychology. https://positivepsychology.com/gratitude-exercises/

Pomfrey, E. (n.d.). Eat, meditate, exercise—treating anxiety naturally. Transcendental Meditation. https://www.tm.org/resource-pages/211-eat-meditate-exercise

Power Of Positivity. (n.d.). 5 Signs of a "real" positive person. https://www.powerofpositivity.com/5-signs-of-a-real-positive-person/

Roberts, E. (September 13). How to reduce social anxiety and increase self-confidence. Hartstein Psychological. https://www.hartsteinpsychological.com/reduce-social-anxiety-increase-self-confidence

Ross, F. (2018, June 8). Stress vs. anxiety—knowing the difference is critical to your health. Mental Health First Aid. https://www.mentalhealthfirstaid.org/external/2018/06/stress-vs-anxiety/

Salzgeber, N. (2018, July 8). 8 Gratitude exercises to unlock the most powerful emotion that exists. NJ Lifehacks. https://www.njlifehacks.com/gratitude-exercises/

Scott, E. (2019, July 8). The benefits of cultivating gratitude for stress relief. Very Well Mind. https://www.verywellmind.com/the-benefits-of-gratitude-for-stress-relief-3144867

Scott, E. (2019, June 14). How positive thinking impacts your stress levels. Very Well Mind. https://www.verywellmind.com/how-does-positive-thinking-impact-your-stress-level-3144711

Scott, E. (2020, January 24). How to relieve stress with art therapy. https://www.verywellmind.com/art-therapy-relieve-stress-by-being-creative-3144581

Scott, E. (2020, July 20). Reduce stress and improve your life with positive self talk: Develop the positive self talk habit! Very Well Mind. https://www.verywellmind.com/how-to-use-positive-self-talk-for-stress-relief-3144816

Scott, E. (2020, June 27). How to get organized to manage stress. Very Well Mind. https://www.verywellmind.com/tips-on-getting-organized-3145158

Scott, E. (2020, June 29). Art activities for stress relief: These art activities are proven by research to relieve stress. Very Well Mind. https://www.verywellmind.com/art-activities-for-stress-relief-3144589

Scott, E. (2020, June 29). The main causes of stress: What impacts you most may not be the same as for someone else. Very

Well Mind. https://www.verywellmind.com/what-are-the-main-causes-of-stress-3145063

Scott, E. (2020, March 30). The benefits of yoga for stress management. Very Well Mind. https://www.verywellmind.com/the-benefits-of-yoga-for-stress-management-3145205

Segal, J., Smith, M., Segal, R., & Robinson, L. (2020, May). Stress symptoms, signs, and causes. Help Guide. https://www.helpguide.org/articles/stress/stress-symptoms-signs-and-causes.htm

Staff Author. (2020, January 6). How to identify & attract positive friendships. My Domaine. https://www.mydomaine.com/benefits-of-positive-friends-1384779

Stillman, J. (2017, March 27). 8 Types of toxic people who will rob you of your happiness: Science shows even small doses of toxic people can do outsize damage to your life. Inc. https://www.inc.com/jessica-stillman/8-types-of-toxic-people-you-should-always-avoid.html

Stress Hack. (n.d.). Positive thinking: Reduce stress and enjoy life more. http://www.stresshack.com/positive-thinking.html

Tartakovsky, M. (2018, July 8). 3 Art therapy techniques to deal with anxiety. Psych Central. https://psychcentral.com/blog/3-art-therapy-techniques-to-deal-with-anxiety/

Team Tony. (n.d.). How to surround yourself with good people: 10 quotes to inspire you to surround yourself with good people. Tony Robbins. https://www.tonyrobbins.com/stories/business-mastery/surround-yourself-with-quality-people/

This Way Up. (n.d.). I feel shy. https://thiswayup.org.au/how-do-you-feel/shy/

Toney, R. (2019, October 23). 5 Reasons you need to get rid of all your negative friends. Everyday Power. https://everydaypower.com/why-get-rid-of-negative-friends/

ULifeline. (n.d.). Good stress, bad stress: How do you tell the difference between good stress and bad? http://www.ulifeline.org/articles/450-good-stress-bad-stress

University of Nevada, Reno. (n.d.). Releasing stress through the power of music. https://www.unr.edu/counseling/virtual-relaxation-room/releasing-stress-through-the-power-of-music

Voltolina V. (2017, December 6). 3 Easy tricks to get organized and reduce stress. Huffpost. https://www.huffpost.com/entry/organization-and-stress_n_5851704?guccounter=1

WebMD. (2020, March 9). Causes of stress. https://www.webmd.com/balance/guide/causes-of-stress#1-2